# WINDOWS
## *on Stewardship*

Erika Puni, Ph.D.

Written by Erika Puni, Ph.D.

Edited by Sandra Blackmer

Copyright ©2015

Publication number STW 4040
A General Conference Stewardship Ministries Department Publication

ISBN 978-0-9912711-2-2

This material may be translated, printed, or photocopied by any Seventh-day Adventist entity without securing further permission. Republished documents must include the credit line: Stewardship Ministries Department, General Conference of Seventh-day Adventists, used with permission. Selling this work for profit is prohibited.

Unless otherwise noted, all Bible texts are taken from the New International Version. Texts credited to NIV are from the Holy Bible, New International Version®, NIV® Copyright © 1973, 1978, 1984, 2011 by Biblica, Inc.™ Used by permission. All rights reserved worldwide.

Texts credited to NKJV are from the New King James Version. Copyright © 1979, 1980, 1982 by Thomas Nelson, Inc. Used by permission. All rights reserved.

Stewardship Ministries Department
General Conference of Seventh-day Adventists
12501 Old Columbia Pike
Silver Spring, MD 20904, USA

gcstewardship@gc.adventist.org
www.adventiststewardship.com
www.Facebook.com/Dynamicstewards
Issuu.com/dynamicstewards
Vimeo.com/GCStewardship

Printed by Pacific Press Publishing Association, PO Box 5353, Nampa, ID 83653-5353

# FOREWORD

For many, stewardship is the name of a department. For some, the director and those who work with him are the "money people." For Dr. Erika Puni, however, stewardship is not limited to a bank account or to an offering plate. Stewardship for him is a total life experience with Jesus. It certainly includes resources such as our finances, but at its heart, stewardship is about a response to God's generosity, about our service to Him and others because of what God has already done. Stewardship isn't about getting God to do more. It is all about our desire to give our all to Him as our Lord and Savior.

For more than four years I have worked with Dr. Puni as one of his associates and as the editor of the *Dynamic Steward*. During this time we have traveled to all corners of the globe, presented seminars together, and even cried and laughed together. We have become more than work colleagues; we have become friends. By going through these experiences together I have seen him not only preach stewardship but also live it. His effervescent personality has brought stewardship from the textbook into the family circle. Stewardship, as he would say, is a wholistic experience and has an appeal for both adults and children.

This book, *Windows on Stewardship*, contains nearly 10 years of articles that he has written for the *Dynamic Steward*. Yes, the articles reflect his role as director of the Stewardship Ministries Department, but they also reflect his deep personal concerns for people and for their faithfulness and their need to sense an accountability to Christ and those for whom He gave Himself. As the editor of the *Dynamic Steward*, I invite you to read the following pages not just for their content but also as a revelation of the man who wrote them.

Larry R. Evans, D.Min.
General Conference Associate Stewardship Director
Editor of the *Dynamic Steward*

# INTRODUCTION

*Windows on Stewardship* is a compilation of short concept articles that I have penned over the last 10 years for *Dynamic Steward*, the quarterly journal of the Stewardship Ministries Department of the General Conference of Seventh-day Adventists. In the context of the journal, these articles were meant to provide a particular "frame" and window of understanding into this broad and rich biblical concept of stewardship, focusing on each edition's theme. As a religious educator and student of the Bible, I've come to understand stewardship to be a Christian experience and reality that is all-inclusive and encompassing of all of the work of God in one's life. Of course, it's a personal choice and response from the heart, but it is also the work of God in us and for us. "Stewardship is all of me in response to all of God."

With this wholistic understanding of stewardship, I want to introduce you, the reader and a fellow traveler, to other aspects of God's management in our lives as stewards of His kingdom. You will see and experience these under the different chapters and articles, which are organized chronologically. Yes, stewardship includes our financial responsibility to God and others, but it involves much more than money. It is really about living life under the rule of Jesus Christ—both our Savior and Lord (Matt. 6:33). More important, stewardship is about "being" in relationship with Christ daily and allowing Him to transform us from within. "Apart from me you can do nothing" (John 15:5).

*Windows on Stewardship* is devotional in content and spiritual in orientation. This is a journey of exploration where one is invited and encouraged to discover different aspects and dimensions of Christian stewardship. But this is also a call to action: to live and act as God's stewards and trustees in the world. This is our spiritual calling and responsibility. "And God said 'Let us make man in our image, in our likeness, and let them rule over the fish of the sea and the birds of the air, over the livestock, over all the earth, and over all the creatures that move along the ground" (Gen. 1:26). Stewardship is a divine call to the church and to all peoples of the world.

To enhance your journey and help you appreciate more of the different stewardship vistas that you will discover throughout the pages of this book, we're also providing for you visual imagery in each article, a window to enrich your experience. Enjoy the view!


Erika F. Puni, Ph.D.
Stewardship Ministries Director
General Conference

# ACKNOWLEDGEMENTS

Ministry is never done in a vacuum or in the absence of a team of colleagues or without the support of family members and friends. These are persons whom God brings into one's life to inspire, encourage, support, and create an environment that is conducive to spiritual growth. All of this maximizes ministry effectiveness in the service of God.

As a child and later a young person growing up in the "mission fields" of the South Pacific, my life was influenced and molded to a large extent by the example of my parents, the late Pastor Fereti and Mrs. Puataunofo Puni. What I am today as a person and a pastor, and what I do today as a stewardship educator for the General Conference, is the realization of their fervent prayers and parental influence. I dedicate this book to their memory and to their commitment to the kingdom of God.

My life of service at the General Conference for the past 10 years has been made easy because of the faithful support of my wife and partner in ministry, Maxine, and our two children, Janae-Grace and Jaydon. Their love and constant prayers as I travel the world to share principles of Christian stewardship and help people experience Christ at the deepest level, have been a great source of strength for me, and this collection of stewardship perspectives is also a tribute to them.

Space does not allow me to mention all those persons—friends and ministry colleagues—who, in one way or another, have played important supporting roles in my growth and service for God. To all of them I say thank you. In a special way, I want to acknowledge the work of our *Dynamic Steward* editorial team under the leadership of Claire Eva, Maria Ovando-Gibson, and Larry Evans, with whom I had the pleasure and privilege of working during the last 10 years. This book, of course, would not have happened without the persistent encouragement of Johnetta Flomo, administrative assistant for the department, and Penelope Brink, assistant director, technical advisor, and coordinator for this project. To you, my team, thank you.

## SENIOR STEWARDS:
*Passing the Torch*

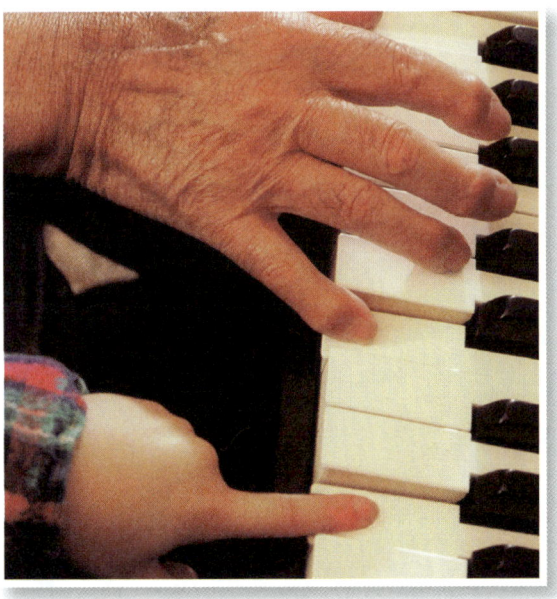

# TO SERVE FOR LIFE

### *Number in the Thousands*

We see them in airports, hospitals, shopping malls, and other public places, giving volunteer service and support to various government entities and nonprofit organizations. At the Auckland International Airport in New Zealand, for example, they are known as the women and men in blue because of the color of their jackets. They may be staffing the information booth, or simply giving directions to visitors and travelers who are looking for a particular office, shop, or transport pick-up area.

These senior stewards number in the thousands anywhere in the world, providing crucial service and help to local authorities and community agencies whose resources are already stretched to the limit. These teams of retirees and seniors save their adopted organizations and beneficiaries thousands, even millions of dollars every year through their dedication and life of service to humanity.

## A Caring Neighbor

In Woongarrah, New South Wales, Australia, I know him as John Ball. He is my neighbor, an Anglican Christian, a retired soldier, and a caring citizen of our local neighborhood. When John sees weeds such as bindii and clover in my front lawn, he sprays them without hesitation or question. For John, this act of kindness is what neighbors do.

When we are away for a few days or a prolonged period of time, he checks the mailbox for unsolicited advertising and newspapers and takes them away. On numerous occasions when I have been traveling within the South Pacific or abroad, he and his wife, Kester, have extended invitations to my wife, Maxine, to stay with them until I returned. John and Kester are good examples of senior stewards, people who understand the principles of giving and looking after people in community.

## Mentors and Friends

In Cooranbong, Australia, where Avondale College is located, I know him as Pastor Austin Fletcher—retired minister and former theology lecturer at the college. Austin was one of a number of retired pastors whom the Faculty of Theology called to assist with the field education component of the ministerial program offered at Avondale during my time of teaching there.

The primary task assigned to Austin and his retired friends who resided at the local Adventist Retirement Village was mentoring for the first-year theology students. These men did more than what was expected of them. They were mentors, counselors, tutors, and friends to the students under their care. They shared their ministerial experience with them, giving generously of their time and resources and opening their homes and hearts in support of these young and upcoming leaders of the church. Austin was truly a senior steward of God's kingdom.

## She Served Others

I knew her in New Zealand as a woman with a heart for the poor and the underprivileged. She is Margaret Jackson from the Cambridge Adventist Church, North New Zealand Conference. Margaret had been involved with the church's Community and Welfare Service for many years, known as the "Dorcas Society." She has been a member of the New Zealand Bible Society, teaching Bible in public schools as well as a class in floral art. She helps with the Citizen's Advice Bureau, and is a campaigner against alcohol. For five years she was president of the Women's Christian Temperance Union (WCTU) for New Zealand and one-time president for the world organization. Margaret is a senior steward working in partnership with God in the use of her gifts—making an effort to make a difference in the lives of people that she meets.

## *A Common Thread*

So what do these individuals have in common? John, Austin, and Margaret all believe in giving of themselves in service to others. Their commitment to doing good in the community is part and parcel of their worship and their lifestyle as stewards of God's kingdom on earth. Their love for God results in their love for people. They understand the principles of biblical stewardship that call for men and women everywhere to give fully of themselves as Christ gave His all for us.

These three stewards represent many people in the world who believe that service is for life. And like Joshua, a senior steward and leader of Israel, their lives stand as a witness and challenge to the rest of us that a life of service to others really matters.

# CONTENTMENT:
## *Pure Contentment*

# CONTENTMENT IN GOD

Our baby daughter, Janae-Grace, is only 3 months old, and she has already shown us signs of contentment. Provided her nappy is dry and she has had her sleep and feeding, she is a very happy child. She can be awake and left by herself for a few minutes and be quite content while we are doing something else. Just today, some friends took us out for lunch, and they commented, "She is a very contented baby." They remarked about her healthy skin, smiling face, and cheerful expressions. As parents, we took their comments to mean that our baby's needs are being met; she is satisfied, comfortable, and relaxed. Contentment is a quality of life expected by God's children.

## *Contentment in God's Covenant of Love*

Included in the Ten Commandments given to Israel at Sinai is the tenth command, which calls for God's people to be satisfied with the blessings God Himself gives them (Exod. 20; Deut. 5). Interestingly, like the other nine, this commandment is in the context of a God who had invited Israel to be in a covenant relationship with Him (Exod. 19:5, 6). They were to be His special people in the world. In Exodus 20, contentment is an experience and consequence that is made possible because of connectedness to God.

Another significant aspect of contentment for the people of Israel was the awareness that God had already saved them (Exod. 20:1, 2), and as such, He expected them to be content with what they received from Him through grace (Exod. 20:17). More important, contentment is an expression of our worship of God and a demonstration of our love toward our neighbors.

## *Contentment in the Sustaining God*

The psalmist David was content with God when he said, "The Lord is my shepherd, I shall not want" (Ps. 23:1, KJV). In this psalm, he pictures himself as a sheep—feeding in green pastures; drinking from a quiet, slow-flowing stream; being watched over by the "Good Shepherd." To David, the psalm was a hymn of gratitude and testimony to a God who provides and sustains daily. It is a psalm about a God who always watches and protects His flock. It is the story of the Almighty, who reaches out to His people in all generations and blesses them because of His everlasting love. Psalm 23 is a promise of God's divine providence, His protective power, and His constant presence with David then and with us today.

## *Contentment in God's Rulership*

The disciples had been with Jesus—their teacher and mentor—as observers and ministry assistants, but the time had now come for them to live out the principles of His kingdom. "Blessed are the poor in spirit, for theirs is the kingdom of heaven. Blessed are those who mourn for they will be comforted. Blessed are those who hunger and thirst for righteousness, for they will be filled" (Matt. 5:3, 4, 6).

In this sermon, Jesus clearly demonstrates how God deals with people who are in relationship with Him. He blesses them before He asks for a love response from them. Moreover, the sense of well-being, inner peace, and contentment experienced by the disciples, in spite of the pressing challenges of the world outside, is a reflection of a life that is under the control and lordship of Jesus Christ.

The willing submission of the disciple's heart to the will of God (as taught by Jesus in the above passage) is what stewardship and discipleship are all about. It is practical Christian living—for discipleship means surrendering self fully to God. What matters is not just giving Him our resources, time, and skills; it is releasing all we have in Him to Him, including our hearts. Contentment is trusting God, no matter what the cost. It is living out the principles of stewardship where Jesus is Lord over all.

## *Contentment and the Will of God*

A key element of the Lord's Prayer that Christ taught the disciples is the double emphasis on God's "kingdom" and "will" (Matt. 6:10). Both concepts speak to the one reality: that God must rule supremely. For Jesus, this desire to live the life of the Father was paramount in all He did during His earthly ministry. At Gethsemane, when He struggled alone while His associates were asleep, His commitment to this divine purpose was demonstrated as He prayed, "My Father … your will be done" (Matt. 26:42). And even on the cross of Calvary, where He suffered death as the Savior of the world, He continued to trust God with these words, "Father, into your hands I commit my spirit" (Luke 23:46).

Contentment for Jesus is living the will of His Father, always. But what about us, His stewards and people today? Are we willing to live out His will in our life and in service for Him?

## DISCIPLES IN THE WORLD:
*Will You Go Where He Leads?*

# GROWING DISCIPLES IN THE WORLD

Spring is the time for new life, rejuvenation, new growth, and new beginnings; and there is no better picture of this change in season than the cherry blossoms of Washington, D.C., capital of the United States. On the day we visited in April, thousands of cherry trees lining the lake were all blossoms—flowers of pink and white—quite a scene to behold. The cherry blossom is evidence that the trees, in spite of their leafless appearance, are still alive and growing.

The church, the community of God's people in the world, is like cherry trees. It is a living organism, and God expects it to grow. In fact, growth is a natural manifestation of anything that is alive. But how do you grow the church? The church grows when members are spiritually connected to Jesus Christ, and as disciples they, in turn, go out and introduce others to Him.

As the General Conference Stewardship Department, we believe in a growing church. Because of this, we chose "Growing Disciples in the World" as our theme for the 2006 World Advisory. This decision to focus on growing disciples is not only consistent with our philosophical understanding of biblical stewardship, but also demonstrates our commitment to the "Tell the World" initiative of the General Conference. Of the seven goals identified as focus areas for the initiative (see Stewardship Window, p. 5), I want to address two—spiritual growth and personal witness—that we can contribute toward in our stewardship ministry around the globe.

## *Spiritual Growth and "Tell the World"*

The intent of this goal is to increase the percentage of Seventh-day Adventist members in the world who are engaged in daily, personal Bible study and prayer. But why is such an emphasis important for the individual church member and corporate church? Daily Bible study and prayer are essential food for spiritual growth. It is the fruit of the life that is connected to Christ. In the Christian walk, we study the Word of God because in it we find Jesus, the "Living Word" (John 5:39). It is in the Bible that we discover the will of God for ourselves and are confronted with the person of Christ, whom to know is life eternal. It is in the study of the Scriptures that God will change our mind-set and our behavior (Luke 24:32-35).

But Bible study in the context of this world initiative is more than what we do for personal devotion or for the purpose of understanding an issue or query. We study the Word to know and experience Jesus as our personal Savior and Lord, and this is Christian stewardship. As Seventh-day Adventists, we must commit ourselves to this goal as a matter of lifestyle. Moreover, this spiritual goal has to be part of our ongoing stewardship education in the churches.

In the real world of Christian living, Bible study is the natural partner to prayer. They go together like hand and glove. In the context of spiritual growth, prayer is both communion and communication with God. It is talking to Him as our Father and listening to Him daily. But more important, it is being in the presence of the Almighty. In the words of Ellen White, "Prayer is the opening of the heart to God as to a friend"(*Steps to Christ*, p. 93). Prayer is a gift from God and the lifeline that connects us to Him 24/7. It is the breath that gives life to our soul, and, in this sense, prayer is critical to being alive in Christ and fundamental to being a disciple and steward of God.

## *Personal Witness and "Tell the World"*

Personal witness as a goal of Tell the World is a challenge to 5 million Seventh-day Adventists to reach at least one person for Jesus and to bring them into fellowship with the church by the year 2010. This goal of 5 million is established to encourage Adventists to participate in God's mission, but it is also a reminder to every church member that by accepting Jesus as our personal Savior and Lord, we are under obligation to God to share His love with everyone we come in contact with. It is important to note, however, that the challenge is to church members and not to pastors or professional evangelists, and the reason for this broad appeal is clear. Christ's mandate to His church to make disciples of all peoples (Matt. 28:18-20) is an invitation to every believer and member—and pastors and evangelists are included. Involvement in personal witness is based on our relationship with Jesus and our responsibility as stewards and disciples. Personal witness is the lifestyle of the Christian and an expression of biblical stewardship.

## *Our Personal Involvement With "Tell the World"*

While I have limited the discussion of Tell the World to two areas, the other five are also important in fulfilling God's mission in the world. My intention was to simply identify two of these goals where I see the stewardship ministry of the church playing a major part in implementing this world initiative. My prayer for the reader is this: "God, help me to recognize the value of growing together with You in prayer and Bible study. Use me as an instrument of Your grace to share Your love with others every day."

# SERVICE:
## *While Life Happens, Serve As You Go*

# "TO SERVE OR NOT TO SERVE"

"Good morning, Sir. This is a courtesy call from your Ford dealer, checking to see if you are happy with the car service you received from us a couple of days ago." Indeed, I was happy and impressed to hear from my local dealer, knowing that they care about me—the customer. In a hotel where we stayed recently, there was no microwave to sterilize Janae-Grace's bottles and no electric kettle for her hot water, but room service was willing to deliver us boiled water daily, for a fee. The hotel support staff was definitely willing to help, but it cost three dollars to deliver hot water to our room!

In Australia, where we had lived for some time, and in our new country of residence, the United States of America, I am encouraged to learn of the growing number of individuals and organizations that are involved in local and international volunteering—a special kind of service commitment. As followers of Jesus in 2006, I wonder if we would be willing to serve Him in the refugee camps of Darfur, Sudan; in the crime-infested favelas (slums) of Rio de Janeiro, Brazil; or in the underserviced areas of New Orleans. This is the question.

## *Serving, Bottom Up*

As humans with carnal natures, the disciples of Jesus did not comprehend the centrality of "service" to the kingdom or rule of God. Their thoughts and attitudes were influenced by the secular agenda of their time—position, self, and the desire to be served by others. And when the issue of leadership surfaced within the circle of the twelve, Jesus had to confront this selfish craving for the "number one" position by saying: "You know that the rulers of the Gentiles lord it over them, and their high officials exercise authority over them. Not so with you. Instead, whoever wants to become great among you must be your servant, and whoever wants to be first must be your slave—just as the Son of Man did not come to be served, but to serve, and to give his life as a ransom for many" (Matt. 20:25-28).

For Jesus, His kingdom's manifesto is service, and this emphasis is contrary to the philosophical position of the world. On this occasion, Christ made it explicitly clear that for anyone to be part of His community—His people—they must live by this service principle. But the test of discipleship is not simple, because it calls for the emptying of self and for one to take on the role of a slave, a position that society accepts as lower than a hired servant. Slaves have no legal rights, no special privileges, no defense when abused by their masters, and no future but to work and serve at the mercy of their owners. But to be sure the disciples now understand His purpose and mission in the world, Jesus illustrates the point with His own life: "The Son of Man did not come to be served, but to serve."

## *With Basin and Towel*

It was the celebration of Passover and their last supper together before the cross, and Jesus wanted to spend this time alone with His disciples (John 13). But the place for this evening meal did not belong to anyone in the group, so there was no host, and, consequently, there were no servants or slaves around to do the menial task of washing the guests' feet before entering and eating. Given the uniqueness of the situation, who should be serving in this incidence? Culturally, it cannot be Jesus. He is the master and leader, and He holds the place of respect among the group. But no one offers, and not one of the twelve is willing to initiate the custom of foot washing.

Again, Jesus, Lord of the universe, has to demonstrate once more that living under the rule of God means serving even as a servant. But there is more to serving! For Jesus, service is a mark of true discipleship (John 13:14, 15). Furthermore, the person who serves with the basin and towel will be blessed by God (John 13:17).

## *A Serving Attitude*

Service as an outward behavior—what is seen by people—is an expression of an attitude of mind and heart. The apostle Paul makes this point when writing to the Galatian Christians: "Your attitude should be the same as that of Christ Jesus: Who, being in very nature God, did not consider equality with God something to be grasped, but made himself nothing, taking the very nature of a servant, being made in human likeness. And being found in appearance as a man, he humbled himself and became obedient to death, even death on a cross!" (Phil 2:5-8).

Christ's substitutionary death was the ultimate example of service and sacrifice. But while human service is a manifestation of the stewardship of Christian discipleship, such an act of love must spring forth from a heart that is connected to the heart of God Himself. In this way, our service is an extension of Christ's life of service in us and through us. It is not motivated by false humility or prompted by the promise of rewards and personal gains, but a genuine outcome of a life that is ruled by Christ. Service is a Christian lifestyle, an authentic sign of being a disciple of Jesus in the twenty-first century. And so, when our relationship with God is right, then the question about service is no longer "whether to serve or not to serve," but "where and when can I serve?"

## *The Church—A Serving Community*

As members of the body of Christ on earth, where do we start? Let me make a suggestion. I believe that, as Christians, we are called to make a difference for God in the world, but we are to start with our families and friends—those who are near to us and whom we meet regularly. Service is not necessarily a matter of going to faraway places, nor is it determined by how much we give in terms of our resources and time; rather, it is our willingness to make life better for someone in need today.

# STEWARDSHIP:
*In Every Detail, Worship Him ...*

# WORSHIP IS PERSONAL AND COMMUNAL

Worship, like stewardship, is personal and communal. While worship is a personal response of the believer's heart to God for who He is, it is never practiced nor expressed in a vacuum or in isolation from other created beings or communities of people. Take for example my grandmother, Gagau Uelese, who was a member of the Congregational Christian Church of Samoa, formerly known as the London Missionary Society (LMS) in the Samoan Islands. She was a pious Christian who was blind during the time she was living while I was growing up. However, she never failed to offer her morning prayers to God daily. In the context of her open home without walls (Samoan fale) where other family members lived and slept, she would simply sit up (a sign of reverence) inside her mosquito net at the appropriate time according to her body clock and start to sing and then pray.

What always fascinated me as a child at that time was the fact that other family members would follow suit. They would sit up inside their mosquito nets and join the singing and prayer, which started off as a personal exercise but now has taken on a communal function. In this case, the personal (the believer interacting with God) and communal (the community and God relationship) aspects of worship were very much intertwined and affirmed. My grandmother's personal expression of worship impacted my family community's response to God, and the family community validated my grandmother's personal interaction with her God. I must admit that my worship and prayer life were influenced and continue to be challenged by the wonderful example of my grandmother and her worship of God.

## *Worship and Witness—Two Sides of Discipleship*

The Samaritan woman was seeking for the Messiah, and Jesus acknowledges her sincerity by commending her. "But the hour is coming, and now is, when the true worshipers will worship the Father in spirit and truth; for the Father is seeking such to worship Him. God is Spirit, and those who worship Him must worship in spirit and truth" (John 4:23, 24, NKJV). Worship for the woman was initiated in her in a personal journey of discovery with Jesus at the well, but one that she became willing to share with her village people. While the discovery was made in a private encounter with Christ, for her this new experience belonged to the public domain of the village life, thus she became committed to make it known to all who would listen to her. "Come, see a Man who told me all things that I ever did. Could this be the Christ?" (John 4:29, NKJV).

This excitement and joy in meeting the Messiah in person, and her personal testimony to the community, were part and parcel of her new life as a disciple. More important for us, this story clearly demonstrates the personal impact of worship (being found in the presence of Jesus) in the life of a community. "And many of the Samaritans of that city believed in Him because of the word of the woman who testified, He told me all that I ever did. So when the Samaritans had come to Him, they urged Him to stay with them; and He stayed there two days. And many more believed because of His own word" (John 4:39-41, NKJV). This account of worship, conversion, and personal witness suggests for me that as Christians, we could not experience the God of community personally without making positive ripples around us in the lives of people with whom we live and meet daily.

# *Worship Leads to Disciple Making*

The impact of a personal encounter with God always leads to worship, and this spiritual experience was certainly true of the disciples when Jesus appeared to them after the Resurrection. "When they saw him, they worshiped him; but some doubted. Then Jesus came to them and said, 'All authority in heaven and on earth has been given to me. Therefore go and make disciples of all nations, baptizing them in the name of the Father and of the Son and of the Holy Spirit, and teaching them to obey everything I have commanded you" (Matt. 28:17-20, NIV). Worship for the disciples was a natural response to the self-revelation of Jesus Christ as Lord of life. Not only was He raised from the grave and the grip of death by the power of God, but now because of His resurrection He ruled supremely as the sovereign Lord of heaven and earth.

Of great significance in this post-Resurrection account is the fact that the disciples' worship experience did not end with worship per se; but rather it provided the motivation and impetus for the next important phase in their lives as followers of Jesus—to witness and make new disciples for Him. This dual emphasis of worship and witness is fundamental to the church being the community of God. The personal yearning to know Him intimately as a personal Savior and Lord must lead to a life that is committed to sharing Him with the world. Personal worship and community witness that focus on making disciples are the two sides of the same coin, and Jesus calls for His church to commit to both. These are expressions of Christian stewardship.

## DISCIPLESHIP:
### *Walking, Living, Growing*

# DISCIPLESHIP CHALLENGES

Discipleship is the life of a follower of Jesus and is synonymous with stewardship, a life of personal surrender and commitment to the rule of God in Christ. Both of these biblical emphases imply a lifestyle of absolute trust and faith in Jesus Christ as Lord. But how is this "new" life in Christ lived out in the church, or in the larger community of the world where the church is called to be "salt" and "light"? Quite different, as a matter of fact, and this is the multi-facet challenge that we as the Seventh-day Adventist Church in the twenty-first century are facing. So let me share with you my observations of the challenges and some of the difficulties that confront us as a people.

### *The Challenge of Knowing the Goal*

For some strange reason, what should have been a fairly straightforward command to the church is misunderstood by some Adventists today, and so we have conflicting views about the goal of the Great Commission (Matt. 28:18-

20). Is the church called to make disciples, or are we in the business of simply baptizing people in the absence of a heart commitment to the lordship of Jesus Christ? This misunderstanding and confusion has at times led to many people going through the ritual of baptism but are divorced of a transformed life from within. These church members would gladly wear the "Christian" label with great pride and would openly testify to their new "Adventist" identity, but they have no interest in a lifestyle of service, of sacrifice or personal witness for Christ. In this scenario we are not making disciples, but we're creating a culture of nominal Christianity.

## The Challenge of Information Versus Relationship

Discipleship is not about information or about how much we know of the Bible. Discipleship is all about whom we know and have experienced. For Philip, his personal encounter with Jesus resulted in him saying to Nathanael, "We have found the one Moses wrote about in the Law, and about whom the prophets also wrote—Jesus of Nazareth, the son of Joseph" (John 1:45, NIV). Such a declaration comes not from something that Philip read in the Galilean herald, but a testimony born of meeting Christ personally. The Samaritan woman's discovery of the Messiah, for example, was the result of her being in the presence of Christ Himself (John 4:4-26). Discipleship is about being in relationship with Jesus Christ.

## The Challenge of Post-baptism Teaching

Inherent in Christ's call for the church to make disciples is the emphasis on "teaching them to obey everything" commanded by Christ (Matt. 28:20). But while teaching is recognized as an important component (a means) of the disciple-making process, the question that is frequently asked is, "When should we teach them?" Should the teaching be limited only to what happens before baptism, or should it continue after the event? The sad reality that I have seen in the church is that new members (infants in the faith) are very often left to care for themselves after baptism. There is no post-baptism teaching, no modeling or mentoring, no encouragement or nurturing, and consequently many of them slide back to their old life. So who is responsible for this failure in retaining new converts: the member or the church? While the answer to this question may be complex, such a situation calls for a biblical response that would include the implementation of small-group ministry where members under the leadership of responsible spiritual leaders provide ongoing nurturing and encouragement for all members. Discipleship is a lifestyle of spiritual exploration and discovery, and as such it does not cease with baptism.

## *The Challenge of Biblical Stewardship*

If stewardship is a lifestyle of submission to the lordship of Christ, then believers would willingly give of themselves as partners with God and will take seriously their responsibility as stewards of His gifts and resources. With this biblical understanding of stewardship, I have come to accept that the new life in Christ does not stop with my public declaration of Jesus as Savior and Lord of my life. On the contrary, baptism opens up new vistas of opportunities to express my commitment and love for Him.

## *Where to Go From Here?*

I believe the answer is found in the biblical mandate itself, "make disciples." When the goal is clearly defined, and when the processes of how to make disciples are understood by the church, then we can expect to see lasting results: faithful stewards and a multiplying community of disciples. This community will be characterized by a people with an unwavering love for Jesus, highly committed to personal devotion and Bible study, willing to share their faith with nonbelievers, faithful in corporate worship and in their support of the church, caring for the needs of their families, and always giving of themselves to God and to people in need. I believe this is true discipleship.

# PRAYER:
## *Where Heaven and Earth Touch*

# PRAYER WORKS

Hannah, in her need for a child, called on God, and He rewarded her faith with the birth of Samuel (1 Sam. 1:10, 17, 19, 20, 27). Elijah, in a test of allegiance and worship, called on the Lord, and He brought fire from above that consumed the sacrifice and everything on and around the altar (1 Kings 1:36-39). Daniel and his companions, faced with the reality of death, sought wisdom and deliverance from God, and He answered their prayers even in a foreign land (Dan. 2:17-19). These few examples from the Old Testament are evidence to the power and provisions of God through prayer. Prayer works. It takes us away from the mundane and the ordinary into the presence of the Almighty. But what is the role of prayer in the life of the Christian church today?

## *Prayer and Discipleship*

Prayer was a spiritual fundamental in the life of Israel in the Old Testament, and it was certainly a key component in the lifestyle of the early church, starting with Jesus Christ and the twelve disciples. Prayer was Jesus' communication link to His father during His earthly ministry, and the disciples knew of this spiritual dimension to His life. Not wanting to miss out on the power and peace that come only in connecting with God, one of the twelve came to him one day and said, "Lord, teach us to pray" (see Luke 11:1-13). Significant in Luke's account of this request and the Lord's Prayer in Matthew 6:9-13 is the similarity in the context where Jesus was specifically addressing His disciples. Whereas the model prayer in Luke 11 was a direct response to a need from one of the twelve, the same prayer in Matthew 6 is included as an illustration on how to pray in contrast to the way the "hypocrites" and "pagans" prayed. Prayer is a matter of the heart!

In the Sermon on the Mount, Jesus presents prayer as a heart-to-heart connection with God irrespective of life's situations. It is not about rituals and habits, or about who was looking and listening; prayer is about who we are inside in relation to who God is as our Father. Prayer was not an additional thing to do in a long list of behavioral activities that His followers were to practice daily, but the very heart of what it means to be His disciple in the world. In essence, prayer is presented in both these chapters (Matt. 6 and Luke 11) as integral to the life and ministry of Christ's followers then and even now.

## *Prayer and Healing*

One other important aspect of prayer in the Bible and in the ministry of the early church was the emphasis on praying for the sick. When the son of Elijah's host who provided him with food and shelter fell ill, the prophet prayed to God for healing, and He restored the child to life (1 Kings 17:17-22). This example of Elijah as a man of prayer in the Old Testament was not lost in the eyes of the apostle James, who writing to the scattered community of Christians reminded them of the ministry of praying for the sick. "Is any one of you sick? He should call the elders of the church to pray over him and anoint him with oil in the name of the Lord. And the prayer offered in faith will make the sick person well; the Lord will raise him up. If he has sinned, he will be forgiven" (James 5:14, 15, NIV). Prayer, for James, was not limited only to the realm of worship and witness; rather, it included the area of physical and spiritual healing. Prayer opens up opportunities for Christians to pray and intercede for others within the faith community and outside of the church. Prayer works!

# *Prayer and the Church Today*

Given the prominent place of prayer in the life of God's people in Bible times, I'm led to believe that we, the church, God's people today, would do well to study and apply these experiences of the past to our own ministry journey. I accept that we cannot simply replicate the practices of the past because our situations and contexts are different, but we can certainly capture the spirit and the passion for prayer based on biblical principles contained in the Scriptures. So what are some of these principles that we can incorporate into a prayer strategy for the church in the twenty-first century?

1. Church leaders must model prayer in their own life and ministry as Jesus and the apostles did for their followers in their time.

2. Incorporate prayer into the fabric of church life as a key component of every ministry and activity of the local congregation.

3. Provide opportunity for individuals who see prayer as their spiritual gift, and organize them into a prayer ministry for the church.

4. Make prayer a natural outcome and experience for members who are modern-day disciples of Jesus Christ.

5. Teach prayer as a Christian value and lifestyle issue for believers, focusing on the heart relationship with God and not simply on the forms of prayer.

My hope is that all of us who are involved in ministry for the church will make every effort to connect and stay connected to God as faithful stewards of Christ in our worship and witness for Him daily.

# LIFESTYLE:
## *What Are Your Resources Growing?*

# FINANCIAL STEWARDSHIP: CHRISTIAN LIVING

Biblical stewardship is the acknowledgement of the lordship of Jesus Christ in all areas of the Christian's life. This broad and wholistic understanding of stewardship recognizes that all that we are and all that we have are gifts of God's grace, freely given for our benefit and for the support of His work on earth. One of these precious gifts of God is money—a "medium of exchange" for human services and goods—but its place in the life of the believer is very often misunderstood. So how should a Christian look at finances (the totality of monetary resources) in the context of the consumer-driven and materialistic world we live in? What biblical principles should guide our perspective in relationship to this cultural subsystem of human living, which deals with the accumulation, circulation, and distribution of money and wealth?

# A Biblical Perspective

The Bible provides many practical admonitions and counsel on the subject of finance for God's people, and here are a few selected guiding principles to consider for this edition:

1. Money as a human product and expression of personal finances is a gift of God. While humans have a sinful nature, and while every aspect of life on earth is tainted by sin, not every product of human origin is sinful. To the contrary, the Bible takes the view that money and wealth are blessings of God and can be used for His purposes (Prov. 3:19, 20).

2. Money as a "measure of value" is not evil (as it has no life in itself), nor is it an instrument of the devil. The unguarded want for more money, however, is evil (1 Tim. 6:10). Where money becomes the problem for Christians is when it takes the place of God as the object of personal and corporate worship, which can eventually lead them away from having a relationship with Him.

3. The ability of a person to live within their resources is a sign of spiritual maturity and good financial practice (Prov. 15:16). The opposite, however, is uncontrolled spending and impulse buying, which lead to a life of debt and unnecessary strain and pain on the part of the person and their family. Being content and living on the provisions of God for each day is a sign of responsible Christian living (Exod. 20:17).

4. Saving and investing money for the future is good stewardship. Christians live their lives not just for the present but also in anticipation of the future, which very often is uncertain. For this reason, it is imperative for followers of Christ to put aside something of value for tomorrow (Matt. 6:19).

5. The return of God's tithe and the giving of freewill offerings is part of Christian financial stewardship (Mal. 3:6-8), and it starts with the acknowledgment that God is owner of everything in life. In the disbursement of personal income, God's tithe must be put aside first, followed by the giving of offerings as an expression of gratitude and thanksgiving.

6. Supporting the poor and special projects aimed at developing people in community is part of our spiritual worship. In fact, the care of the poor and the disfranchised of society is a spiritual obligation expected of Christ's people everywhere (Matt. 25:35-40).

7. Financial stewardship includes the proper use and distribution of personal monetary resources in support of God's mission on earth (Matt. 6:20; 28:19, 20). The steward as God's partner will invest in programs and activities that will result in making disciples for His kingdom.

## Living to Give

Sometimes, one of the difficult lessons to learn is living to give and to share one's blessings with others. Jesus, in response to a question on inheritance and possessions, told this parable of the rich fool (Luke 12:13-21), and made His point clear to His disciples that life is not about the "abundance of possessions" (Luke 12:15); it is about knowing God and His purpose in one's life (Luke 12:21). Beyond this primary emphasis of living toward God, Jesus was also illustrating the problem with the rich man's attitude about financial gain as highlighted in the text:

- Personal wealth is not a security or basis for salvation (Luke 12:19).

- God is the constant factor in financial planning (Luke 12:21).

- Jesus expects His disciples to live a life of sharing with others (Luke 12:17).

- Human existence is brief, and death is a reality (Luke 12:20).

## Trust Is the Essence

In addressing the issues of investment, money, and finances in the Sermon on the Mount (Matt. 6:19-34), Jesus made some very important comments to His disciples that are also applicable to His followers today:

1. "For where your treasure is, there your heart will be also" (Matt. 6:21, NIV). Jesus recognized the power of money and wealth, and is making the point that finances have influence on the human heart, and very often the heart will follow earthly treasures. The question for us is "Where is your heart?"

2. "No one can serve two masters. Either he will hate the one and love the other, or he will be devoted to the one and despise the other. You cannot serve both God and money" (Matt. 6:24, NIV). Christ is making a commitment call by asking all His followers this question, "Whom will you worship, God or money?"

3. "But seek first his kingdom and his righteousness, and all these things will be given to you as well" (Matt. 6:33, NIV). These words are both a promise and a plea. "I will bless you financially, but I want to have a relationship with you. I want to come into your heart!"

4. "O you of little faith" (Matt. 6:30, NIV). The bottom line in the matter of Christian living is whether we can trust God with our whole life, including our finances, and whether we will allow Him to be an active partner in our financial planning. More important is the issue of personal relationship and connectedness with Him daily. Will you let Him be the Lord of your life today?

# MINISTRY:
## *Living God's Vision—His Call to Journey*

# BASIC CHRISTIANITY AND STEWARDSHIP

The book of Acts points to Antioch of Syria where the disciples— followers of Jesus Christ—were first called "Christians" (Acts 11:26). This notation, which describes the early believers of Christ, is significant in helping us understand the characteristics of these people who were committed to the way and life of Jesus. In this article I will explore the question, what is a Christian? But I also want to illustrate how biblical stewardship is an expression of Christianity—the lifestyle of a Christian.

## *Understanding the "Christian" Context*

Acts 11:26 is the first of three Bible texts (Acts 26:28; 1 Pet. 4:16) that uses the term "Christian." It is in looking at the totality of Acts 10 and 11 that we can see clearly the broad meanings carried by this name for followers of Christ in the first century. Note the following observations from the biblical text:

1. Acts 11 uses the word "Christians" as a synonym for these other terms: "disciples" (11:26), "witnesses" (10:39), and "brothers" (11:1). The use of "disciples" with "Christians" in the same verse conveys the idea that Christians were students and followers of Jesus Christ. He was their Master and Teacher, and they followed His teachings. "Witnesses" was Peter's preferred term to explain the role of the twelve who spent time with Jesus during His earthly ministry from His baptism to His ascension and including the historical event of His resurrection (Acts 1:21; 10:39-41). Peter's point in this testimony is that "witnesses" have an intimate knowledge and personal experience with Jesus. "Brothers," on the other hand, is Luke's picture that depicts the apostles (the twelve key leaders of the church at Jerusalem) as a close-knit community of people, and this was certainly the case with the first twelve, who shared a common life with Christ. While the emphasis of the term "Christians" is on the aspect of following, the word definitely has elements of acknowledging the lordship and messiahship of Jesus—He is the "anointed" and "appointed" of God (Acts 10:36, 38, 42).

2. Another key observation that provides richness to the use of the word "Christians" in the context of Acts 10 and 11 is Peter's acknowledgment that God has no favorite people, and He accepts "all" persons regardless of their place of origin. For Peter, Christians comprise individuals from "every nation" (Acts 10:34-36, 45; 11:1, 18), even those from outside of the Jewish society.

3. The most important observation that stands out in the context of these two chapters is the connection between "Christians" and the gospel commission—the making of disciples for Jesus (Acts 10:33, 47; 11:21, 24; Matt. 28:19, 20). In Acts 10 we see the three modes of making disciples (go, teach, baptize). In Matthew 28 this commission comes together in Peter's ministry to Cornelius at Caesarea; while Acts 11 records the spread of the gospel to other areas outside of Jerusalem (Antioch included).

4. One final point that we must not overlook is the offering of prayers and the giving of gifts by Cornelius (Acts 10:31), and the receiving of the gift of the Spirit by the Gentiles (vss. 45-47). This aspect of giving is also noted in the life of the church at Antioch, where disciples gave gifts to Barnabas and Paul in support of other Christians (11:27-30). Christianity is about sharing the good news of Jesus (vs. 20) and giving to people in need.

## Fundamentals of Christianity

Our brief analysis of the Acts passages reveals the following features of early Christians:

1. Christians know Jesus Christ personally and have an intimate relationship with Him.

2. Christians believe and acknowledge that Jesus is divine, and that He is the anointed of God—the Messiah.

3. Christians follow the teachings of Jesus in the Bible in both words and deeds, and they value time of devotion with Him in prayer.

4. Christians are mandated to be involved in God's mission in the world to make disciples of all peoples. They are "witnesses" of the risen Lord.

5. Christians have open hearts that accept people of different color and culture into their fellowship and community—the church. They are "brothers," individuals who possess love and affection for Christ and other Christians.

6. Christians as a matter of lifestyle give generously in support of God's cause, which includes the needs of the poor in the world.

## Stewardship and Christianity

On the basis of our study we can conclude that the word "Christianity" is synonymous with the biblical concept of stewardship for the following reasons:

1. Stewardship is about an experience with the person of Jesus Christ: Creator, Owner, and Redeemer. It's about knowing Him personally as Savior and Lord.

2. Christian stewardship has to do with having an intimate, ongoing, and continuous relationship with Him.

3. Stewardship is about obedience to God and the teachings of Jesus as revealed in all of His Word, the Bible. Such obedience is manifested in the Christian appropriating time for Bible study and prayer.

4. Christian stewardship raises awareness of the spiritual obligation of Christians to make disciples, which results in personal involvement in witnessing and evangelism.

5. Stewards live the principles of God's kingdom, which promote acceptance of all peoples regardless of their social status and ethnicity.

6. Christians recognize that all of life, including our earthly possessions, are gifts of God given freely to serve Him and to help others. The Christian's purpose in life is to honor and glorify God in all things.

# TIME:
## *An Invisible Gift—A Chance to Choose*

# TIME ALONE WITH GOD

Human life is lived out in segments of time. Whether one is engaged in church ministry or in personal activities, in corporate events, or individual pursuits of life, all of our human endeavors take place in time. This reality means that none of us can afford to squander this precious gift and resource of God in the way we conduct ourselves in the world. Even the "preacher" in the wisdom literature recognized the importance of every moment in life by stating, "There is a time for everything, and a season for every activity under heaven" (Eccl. 3:1, NIV).

The importance of time in relationship with God is clearly expressed in Scripture from the very beginning when God instituted the seventh-day Sabbath as a special time when Adam and Eve could experience rest in Him (Gen. 2:1-3). Making time for God in our busy lives is not only "right" in terms of Christian behavior, but it is good stewardship—giving God His rightful place in our lives. God also recognized that humans would need time to revive and survive daily. He created the "night," so His creatures could sleep in order to restore energy and give the body time to do its work of repair and replenish. But more important, God wanted His people to make time to be in communion with Him, so they would come to know Him better as Creator and Savior. Time alone with God is not an option; it is a required discipline of the Christian life.

## *Jesus Made Time*

I find it significant that Matthew, Mark, and Luke all recorded the experience of Jesus in the desert, where He was tested by Satan soon after His baptism. The notation that Jesus was led by the "Spirit" and that He fasted (a spiritual exercise of faith) for forty days during this time, would suggest that He was spending time alone with His Father though tempted by Satan (Matt. 4:1, 2).

In essence, Christ practiced the value of being connected to and in the presence of God as a necessary preparation for service. Not only did He seek time in the beginning of His public ministry for communion with His Father, but He continued to make time for God in His prayer life (Luke 9:18; 11:1). This special time was the secret to His power as manifested in His ministry in Palestine.

## *The Disciples Made Time*

When questioned by the high priest and rulers of the law about the authority by which they healed the crippled man at the temple, Peter testified boldly that it was by the power of Jesus of Nazareth (Acts 4:8-10). The leaders of the temple were amazed with Peter's and John's courage, particularly because they saw them only as ordinary men with no formal education but noted that they "had been with Jesus" (Acts 4:13). Power and courage are the consequences of a life connected to Jesus Christ. The disciples made time for God.

## *Will You Make Time?*

If Jesus felt the necessity of making time for His Father in His life and ministry, and if the twelve disciples saw fit to be in the presence of their Master, thus enabling them to do the impossible, would it not be wise for us as stewards and God's leaders in the church to set aside time for Him today?

# FAMILY FINANCE:
*Dear God, This Belongs To You ...*

# STEWARDSHIP EDUCATION FOR CHILDREN

Many times I have been asked this question in different situations and locations: "When should we start teaching children about tithes and offerings?" The fact that this question is asked frequently suggests an interest on the part of many parents and Christian educators to give children proper training in this very important aspect of their spiritual development. For church members to ask this question would indicate their awareness of the value of childhood education in the formation of Christian values and good behavior. There is also a consensus on the part of many that this process needs to be implemented very early in the child's life, and I agree.

Whenever I am presented with this question, my mind always goes to this text of Scripture: "Fix these words of mine in your hearts and minds; tie them as symbols on your hands and bind them on your foreheads. Teach them to your children, talking about them when you sit at home and when you walk along the road, when you lie down and when you get up. Write them on the doorframes of your houses and on your gates, so that your days and the days of your children may be many in the land that the Lord swore to give your forefathers, as many as the days that the heavens are above the earth" (Deut. 11:18-21, NIV).

## *God's Counsel*

There are several important biblical principles from the Deuteronomy passage cited above that I want to share with our readers in the context of teaching children about God's tithes and offerings:

1. Teaching children about God and His mercy, love, protection, provisions, and blessings is a spiritual responsibility on the part of those who are in a covenant relationship with Him (Deut. 7:8).

2. The Deuteronomy text indicates that spiritual education is about loving God fully with "all your heart and with all your soul" (Deut. 10:12; 11:1). Therefore, the primary task is to help the children to know and experience God personally.

3. Spiritual education includes the teaching of children about the return of tithes and the giving of freewill offerings (Deut. 12:4-6) in recognition of God's creatorship and ownership of everything in the world and the universe (Deut. 10:14). Tithes are returned as an expression of one's faithfulness to God, while the giving of freewill offerings is an act of thankfulness.

4. The framework for teaching children about the giving of tithes and offerings is worship (Deut. 12:4, 11, 12). Worship is acknowledgment of the sovereignty of God and also a demonstration of reverence and love for Him.

5. In the matter of worship and the presentation of tithes and offerings, God expects His people to comply; and He is counting on their obedience that is borne out of love to follow through with His commands (Deut. 11:8, 9; 13-15).

6. When returning tithes or in the giving of freewill offerings, God expects His people to demonstrate a heart of joy and a spirit of cheerfulness (Deut. 12:7, 12).

7. Whereas tithes and offerings are given out of His blessings, God also promises to bless them more after the act of giving to Him (Deut. 11:22-25; 12:20).

## *Stewardship Practice*

The issue in stewardship education for children is not whether we should do it or not; rather, it is about "when," "how," and "what" is the best way to do it. For little children the best way for them to learn about financial stewardship is through their giving in Sabbath School or during the worship service. They obviously do not know the difference between tithes and offerings at this time, but they can learn the value of giving to God through their participation during these important religious activities on Sabbath. At this age their actual doing and our modeling through our own physical giving on a regular basis will communicate to them the importance of giving as an act of worship.

How soon should we begin teaching children? My view is that we can start with them as soon as they are able to see and hold something in their hand. We have done this with Janae-Grace since she was only a few months old, and today at the age of 2 she expects us to give her something to give when we go to church. What about tithes? I am convinced that we can also teach children about tithes very early in their lives once we as parents start to give them money for allowance or when they receive monetary gifts from other people. The little ones are quick learners, and they can be taught to learn that money is a gift and blessing from God, and with this blessing they are expected to return a portion of it to God as a matter of reverence and love for Him.

## SACRED ELOQUENCE:
*Isaiah 55:11, NRSV*

# STEWARDSHIP AND PREACHING

While conducting a stewardship education program in a major city church, a local pastor told me that he had not preached a stewardship sermon in the past two years of his ministry. His reason for not preaching on the subject related to a perceived "conflict of interest" in the minds of some church members. Some members believed the reason why pastors preached on stewardship was because they were paid from tithe funds. If this was the only reason pastors preached and taught on the subject of stewardship, then I would be concerned myself. However, I know that stewardship is more than tithes and offerings.

Stewardship is an all-inclusive response from the believer's heart for all that God has done through His Son, Jesus Christ. Stewardship is about the lordship of Jesus in all areas of our lives as stewards and disciples, and this is why it is imperative for ministers to preach on this subject on a regular basis.

## The Sermon as a Spiritual Tool

In stewardship education, the sermon is a tool for communicating spiritual values and biblical themes to followers of Christ. The potential and capacity of a sermon to influence people's worldviews and core beliefs, for example, are inherent in its very nature as a communication instrument.

However, the sermon is no ordinary means for communicating information. This medium allows for God to speak directly or indirectly to listeners and readers on the basis of His Word, as articulated by the speaker or writer. This is an untapped power of influence that pastors and lay leaders could use to a great effect in promoting stewardship as a Christian lifestyle.

Through the sermon, church members are reminded of their spiritual responsibilities to God as Creator and owner of the universe. Through the sermon, believers are placed in an open field of biblical learning to explore and experience the freshness of God's love in new ways. Through the sermon, God reaches out and touches human hearts in a personal manner. Through the sermon, seekers of truth are affirmed and encouraged in their encounter with God. Through the sermon, followers of Jesus are inspired and challenged to respond to Him in new ways of service and at new levels of sacrifice.

## The Sermon Moves Listeners to Become Doers

Peter's preaching on the day of Pentecost as recorded in Acts 2 has many components of a sermon that are worth noting, particularly its effect on people. The first notable factor is the presence of God in the context and process of the sermon delivery.

The second important factor, as demonstrated in this sermon, was Peter's constant focus and reference to Jesus. This was his subject and purpose for preaching. "Men of Israel, listen to this: Jesus of Nazareth was a man accredited by God to you by miracles, wonders and signs" (Acts 2:22, NIV). "God has raised this Jesus to life, and we are all witnesses of the fact" (Acts 2:32, NIV). "Therefore let all Israel be assured of this: God has made this Jesus, whom you crucified, both Lord and Christ" (Acts 2:36, NIV).

In the sermon, Jesus must be presented to the listening and reading audience as the Incarnate of God and the only answer to our human questioning.

A third significant factor in Peter's preaching is the fact that his sermon was a testimony of his life experience with the living Christ (Acts 2:32). A powerful sermon, therefore, is one where the preacher or writer is telling his or her own story of personal encounter and victory in Jesus.

The fourth factor, and one that is a fundamental of any sermon, is the recognition that this medium of communication has to do with the exposition of the Word of God—the Bible. The sermon is a God-given opportunity to open up the riches of His treasures in Scripture to those who are willing to learn and accept His offer of grace.

It is a spiritual tool that can move individuals from being unbelievers to followers of Christ. In this event, for example, not only were people's hearts convicted by the power of the Holy Spirit (Acts 2:37), but three thousand of them made a life-changing decision to accept Jesus as their Savior and Lord. They were baptized and became members of the church (Acts 2:41). This kind of impact and result can happen only when the Bible is preached and Jesus is lifted up.

# SMALL GROUPS:
*Transformation*

# STEWARDSHIP EDUCATION IN SMALL GROUPS

The utilization of small groups as a ministry tool for evangelism and nurture is a way of doing ministry today; particularly in larger and growing congregations, and in parts of the world where paid workers are few and church members have taken on the role of lay evangelists and pastors. Given its success in introducing people to Jesus Christ, and with its cost effectiveness as a ministry apparatus, I want to focus this article on how to do stewardship education in small groups.

In this discussion I am assuming that it is possible to apply the principles and dynamics of small groups to stewardship education: teaching Christians to live kingdom values in their everyday life. Let me share with you four reasons why I believe small groups can enhance stewardship education in your local church.

## Small Groups—Ideal Opportunity for the Study of Stewardship Principles

The dynamic of fewer persons studying together in a specific time and place provides a unique setting for in-depth study of the Bible. For participants, the small-group situation creates an environment of safety and security where they can be themselves, and for the Bible instructor the small group means a better atmosphere for personal interaction and learning. Let me illustrate. An individual may not feel quite as intimidated in a small group because of the presence of other people as compared to how one may feel in a one-to-one Bible study setting. This aspect of personal comfort is critical in any learning situation, and stewardship education is no exception.

The small group as a learning tool opens up opportunity to communicate stewardship principles in a personal way that is absent in a preaching mode. Group members are free to make observations of the biblical text and ask questions. The instructor can raise issues for discussion, or he may invite participants to reflect on a specific principle and they can respond accordingly if they so desire. This dimension of personal connectedness and direct communication is an important factor in the process of learning biblical truths and in helping people to experience Jesus personally on the basis of His Word.

## Small Groups—Ideal Community for Christian Nurture and Support

The small group naturally leans itself into a way of thinking and doing where group members can be challenged to provide support and care for one another. In this kind of setting, individuals after some time will come to find their identity within the framework of this social unit. They are part of a small faith community. In this new reality, members will learn to accept and trust one another as friends and equals; and this shift in mind-set will in turn help them to open up and share their life journeys, struggles, joys, fears, failures, and victories with the group. With this level of acceptance and openness, group members can now reach out and affirm, encourage, and even pray for one another. Prayer in small groups is a nurturing ministry where members lift up one another into the throne room of heaven, and where God reaches out and touches His people in an intimate and meaningful way.

## *Small Groups—Ideal Fellowship for Sharing Faith Testimonies*

One of the most powerful ways of building faith is through the sharing of personal stories—real-life experiences with God. People as social beings identify with human situations and challenges. Someone's trials and victory over greed, for example, can be the motivating factor for another member to live simply and commit their financial resources fully to the mission of God. The sharing of personal testimonies should be a spontaneous response, which allows for the empowerment of others through another person's encounter with the Divine and their way of dealing with the varying situations in life.

While no pressure must be placed on anyone to share, the host/leader or Bible instructor can encourage participation by inviting certain individuals who are more comfortable in speaking in public to share what God has done for them. Very often, it is the personal testimony from someone's life that moves people from being an unbeliever to a believer and from an unfaithful follower to a committed disciple of Christ. There is no limit to the power and influence of a personal story when it is motivated and directed by the Spirit of God.

## *Small Groups—Ideal System to Practice Accountability*

An invaluable part of small groups, particularly in stewardship education, is the opportunity they provide for members to act as mentors for one another. Mentoring is an accountability system that permits one person to provide support and honest feedback to another individual with the sole purpose of helping them to grow.

This dynamic of personal support and accountability can take place within the context of the group meeting or outside the scheduled group sessions. Accountability contributes to Christian integrity and spiritual maturity. More could be said about other ministry benefits that small groups can bring to stewardship education, but what is more important now is implementation—

giving small groups a go.

It may not work perfectly the first time you try, but practice and persistence may give you the kind of results that you're looking for at this time.

REVIVAL:
*Read—Listen—Live*

# STEWARDSHIP OF GOD'S WORD

What is the place of the Bible in Christian stewardship? Where does the Bible (or the reading and studying of it) fit into the life of Adventist Christians today? Why should church leaders care about how much time church members spend in the study of God's Word? Finally, how will the "Follow the Bible" initiative of the General Conference impact the lives of Adventists across the globe? These questions form the basis of this article, which seeks to highlight the integral relationship between Scripture and stewardship.

## *The Holy Scriptures and Leadership Responsibility*

Seventh-day Adventist leaders at all levels of the church should care about the welfare of our members; after all, we are about personal growth and preparing a people for God's eternal kingdom. Part of our duty of care includes the development of appropriate resources and the initiation of programs to build the body of Christ—the church. With the "Follow the Bible" initiative, our leaders at the General Conference are embarking on a simple ministry idea—to revive our interest and love for the Word of God. In many ways, this is a restatement of a Christian value that we have always had. However, we have come to realize that many of our members today are not studying the Bible on a regular basis, which means that they are not being fed spiritually and are not growing in Christ. "Follow the Bible," therefore, is a church response and ministry initiative to address this weakness in the life of our faith community.

## *The Holy Scriptures and Christian Growth*

The placement of the Bible as the first of twenty-eight fundamental beliefs of Seventh-day Adventists clearly shows the importance and high regard we have for the Word of God. It is a faith statement that testifies to our commitment to the fullness of the Old and New Testaments, and acceptance of the Bible as the standard test for us in matters of biblical truth (doctrines) and Christian experience. This strong emphasis is a reflection of our historical roots as a Protestant movement and church.

Also, beyond our history and statement of Christian beliefs, we take this emphasis on the Bible seriously in the way we do church. For example, we have had since our early beginnings as a Christian organization the Sabbath School program, which promotes daily Bible study and integration of God's Word into the lives of its members (children, youth, and adults). We also have, in addition to the established Sabbath School curriculum, the morning watch booklets and devotional books with daily Bible verses and readings. The purpose behind these devotional and Sabbath School resources is to help our people connect to Jesus and to have a personal experience with Him. We know that it is through the reading and studying of the Word that we can have an encounter with the risen Lord, and as a consequence of this experience grow in our personal lives as Christians.

## *Stewardship Ideas*

The effectiveness of "Follow the Bible" will depend to a larger extent on how we as leaders of the local organizational units of the church promote and engage our people in this initiative. Let me suggest a few ideas that you may want to consider:

1. Reevaluate the way you are doing Sabbath School to ensure that ample time is given Sabbath morning to the actual study of the Bible, including opportunity for discussion, reflection, and integration of Bible truths.

2. Reassess the availability and accessibility of Bible study resources (Sabbath School and devotionals) for your members, and, if necessary, subsidize or provide for persons who may not be able to purchase these resources for themselves.

3. Retool your leaders and members by providing regular training classes on how to study the Bible.

4. Promote family worships and encourage the reading of the Bible as an ongoing activity for all members of the family.

5. Initiate programs and activities in the church, particularly with young people and children, that will create interest in the Bible and the reading of it.

6. Encourage the use and reading of the Bible in your corporate church worship and service.

7. Challenge and involve church members in conducting Bible studies with non-Adventists in their homes and in small groups.

So, why should we study the Bible? "These are the Scriptures" according to Jesus "that testify about me" (John 5:39, NIV).

## *The Holy Scriptures—God's Written Word*

The Seventh-day Adventist Church upholds the Bible as the "written Word of God" (*Church Manual*, 2005, p. 9). As Adventist Christians, we believe the Bible is the "infallible revelation" of God's will and "necessary for salvation" (ibid.). The Bible is the "standard of character, the test of experience, the authoritative revealer of doctrines, and the trustworthy record of God's acts in history" (ibid.). From the perspective of Adventist beliefs, the Bible is part of our church DNA; it's a basic component of our being Adventist!

Christian stewardship, on the other hand, is about living the will of God in the totality of our lives as Christ's disciples. It is allowing God's rule to take hold of us in the ways we relate to people and deal with situations on a daily basis. Our response to God, however, will be influenced and affected by our hearing of His voice as He speaks to us from the pages of Scripture. In this sense, our reading and understanding of the Bible impacts us in the way we live life now as God's people. Being able to read, hear, and understand the Word of God in our cultural contexts is an important Christian discipline of stewardship.

# MONEY MANAGEMENT:
*Financial Courage*

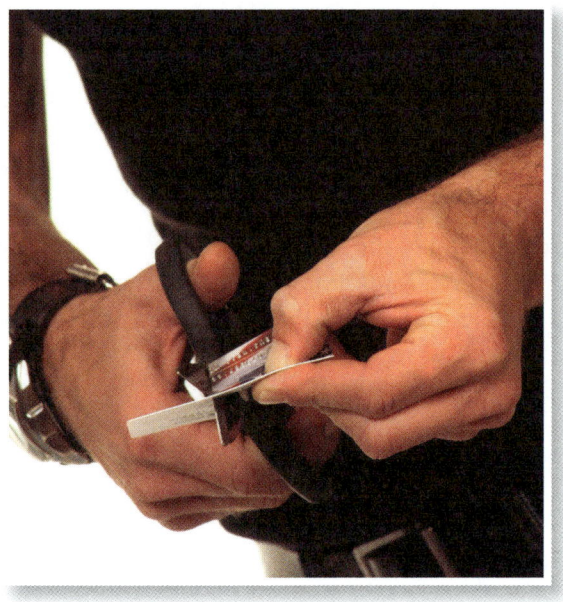

# INVESTMENT, MONEY, AND LIFE

When our family moved to the United States in 2006, we decided to purchase a townhouse. The cost of real estate at that time in the Washington, D.C., area and the surrounding counties was quite high, but prices started to decline soon after. From 2006 until now our property has probably lost value by 10 percent. This loss in our investment is part of the larger financial crisis that is crippling the economy of many countries today and affecting millions of lives around the world. Christians are not immune from this crisis and are looking to Scripture to find answers to this difficult global situation. So let me share some biblical perspectives on this matter from Jesus' Sermon on the Mount (Matt. 5-7).

1. Only one investment is eternally secure. In the cultural context of His time, Jesus made this statement: "Do not store up for yourselves treasures on earth, where moth and rust destroy, and where thieves break in and steal"

(Matt. 6:19, NIV). The "moth" and "rust" imageries communicate pictures of destruction and deterioration, while the "thieves" reference evokes scenes of looting and piracy, which sometimes are accompanied by the loss of human lives. Such is the end result of financial investment that focuses only on this world, where the risk factors are unstable.

2. Given these earthly realities, Jesus then makes the point that His disciples (His primary audience on this occasion) must invest with someone (God) who is trustworthy and in a place (heaven) where their personal investment is secure (Matt. 6:20). It is important to note, however, that Jesus in these Bible verses is not speaking against saving and investing per se; rather, He is contrasting the effects and outcomes of investing on earth and investing in heaven. The choice is ours.

3. Money is only a "means" of worship. "No one can serve two masters. Either he will hate the one and love the other, or he will be devoted to the one and despise the other. You cannot serve both God and money" (Matt. 6:24, NIV). On the surface, these words can be viewed as "hard" because they challenge the hearer toward action and into making a decision either for God or money. But beyond this service decision, Jesus is also calling His disciples into a proper understanding of the use of monetary resources.

Money has its place in the larger scheme of life, but it must not take the rightful place of God as the object of our worship. Unlike God, who is the Creator Himself, money is a service tool created by humans to assist people in the exchange of goods and services. In this sense, money has limited value; it cannot save us or the planet. It has no life! And while it is a "gift" of God, it is only a "means" of worshiping Him.

4. God will provide even in hard times. Jesus recognized the human anxiety of His disciples about the things of this world when He said to them, "Therefore I tell you, do not worry about your life, what you will eat or drink; or about your body, what you will wear" (Matt. 6:25, NIV). And using the objects of their natural surroundings, He assured them that the God of the universe, who provides for the "birds" and the "grass of the field," will also provide for their daily substance and needs. "If that is how God clothes the grass of the field, which is here today and tomorrow is

thrown into the fire, will he not much more clothe you, O you of little faith?" (Matt. 6:30, NIV). In these words, Jesus affirmed to the twelve that they were more important to God than all of nature put together, and they needed to trust Him more. Faith in God is the essence of Christian living.

5. Jesus is the best investment with eternal value. Money has temporal value and benefit and will be affected from time to time by many financial market factors. And like the grass of the field, it will eventually pass away. With this picture in their minds, Jesus called the disciples into a life of surrender to the things of God where Jesus is Lord (Matt. 6:33). Seeking the "kingdom" of God means that the followers of Jesus will allow Him to take control of every facet of their lives, including the management and use of their finances. And even if they don't receive the full benefits of their monetary investment on this side of the Second Coming, or experience great loss as a consequence of living on this planet, they still have Him—and to have Jesus as Savior and Lord is to have everything!

And so, in these times when personal resources are scarce and cash flow is limited; when millions of people are losing jobs and unable to pay their mortgages; when retirement funds once thought of as safe and secured have lost their worth overnight, leaving thousands of contributors uncertain of their life at retirement; when individuals and families lost their lifetime investments through greedy and dishonest investors; there is only one way to turn, and that "Way" is Jesus, who is "the Truth and Life" (John 14:6). With hope diminished in the financial institutions of this world, we are again reminded in these difficult times that the only constant factor in the world is God Himself, who is Creator, Redeemer, Sustainer, and Provider.

# ENVIRONMENTAL STEWARDSHIP:
## *Author—Owner—Creator*

# STEWARDS AS CREATIONISTS AND ADVENTISTS

Growing up as a Seventh-day Adventist on the islands of the South Pacific, I heard very little about Christian responsibility of the environment. On the other hand, we constantly heard sermons and discussions about eschatological events associated with the second coming of Jesus Christ and the millennium, and also of the larger picture of the future ultimate destruction of this world, with God making all things new, including a new heaven and a new earth (Rev. 21). I am not suggesting that as a church community we do not believe in personal responsibility for the earth that we live in, but I am saying that our strong emphasis on the advent of Jesus may have given some people the wrong impression that we care only about going to heaven and have no concern for the environment today. Actually, as Adventists, we believe and teach stewardship of the earth, and we can do more.

"We are God's stewards, entrusted by Him with time and opportunities, abilities and possessions, and the blessings of the earth and its resources. We are responsible to Him for their proper use" (*Seventh-day Adventists Believe*, 2005: 301, 307). In this article, I submit to our readers that Christian stewards are both creationists (believe that Jesus as Creator made all things) and Adventists (believe that Jesus will come back to this earth as King of the universe).

The biblical record begins with the assertion that "in the beginning God created the heavens and the earth" (Gen. 1:1, NIV). This statement of fact makes two very important theological points. First, before anything was made, God was. Second, the universe (the heavens and earth) as we know it is a product of God's creation. Moreover, Adam and Eve (the first humans) were placed by God in the Garden of Eden as partners to extend His "rule" over His creation through their stewardship of the earth (Gen. 1:28; 2:8, 15). Thus, from the very beginning of time, humans were given the special task of being stewards of the world not because they own it but because they accepted God as their maker and owner of all things.

## *Creator and Owner of the Universe*

As a reminder of His sovereignty and ownership of the universe, God in His work of creation set time (the seventh day) aside (made holy) so that Adam, Eve, and their descendants would recognize Him as their Creator. For the first humans, Sabbath keeping was an act of faith in the God who had power to create and in His "completed" work of creation (Gen. 2:1, 2). They did not need to do or add anything more to what God had made, which was "good." The Sabbath was God's invitation for humans to come into His presence to rest and find communion in Him and with Him. Worship, in this context, was both a voluntary and spiritual response to everything that God was and is. Sabbath observance for Adam and Eve was to be an ongoing love experience between them and the Creator, just like their duty to care for the earth.

In response to the question posed by the disciples about the end time and the sign of His coming, Jesus used parables to communicate truths about this subject in Matthew 24 and 25. In the parable of the "talents" (Matt. 25:14-30), Jesus makes the point that persons waiting for the Advent must work and be good stewards of the financial resources given to them by the "Master"

(God). Accountability to God as a steward infers that value and principle are not limited only to money but also to other areas of human life and experience, including care of the environment. This emphasis on personal responsibility and accountability on the part of "Adventists" (individuals waiting for the coming of Jesus as King) is also highlighted in the parable of the "judgment" (Matt. 25:31-46). Jesus' central point in both chapters is that our eschatology of the future must be informed by our theology and life experience of today.

In His last message for the world in Revelation 14, God makes another call for the inhabitants of the earth to honor and worship the Creator "who made the heavens, the earth, the sea and the springs of water" (vs. 7). This reference to the created works of God is not an incidental notation but a significant restatement of who God is. The worship of the Creator God includes the proper care and management of the world that He made. More important, this eternal message of God's good news concludes with the depiction of the return of Jesus as King and coming for the harvest—a time of reckoning and rewards (Rev. 14:14). Our final standing with God at the end time rests on our willingness to acknowledge Him as our Creator, and obedience to His will as revealed in Jesus.

So what do these Bible passages and examples say to us as Christian stewards? They remind us that followers of Jesus are persons who accept His Creatorship and are faithful in their Christian stewardship, which includes proper care and use of the earth's resources, while waiting for Him to come again to reign forever and to make everything new. These individuals live in expectation of the Advent and recognize their God-given responsibility in the present to society and the world they live in. Their hope is for a "new" earth in the future, where the lion and the lamb will roam together and where its citizens live and abide by the laws of the Creator. And this is not in conflict with their present lifestyle of being good and responsible stewards of God's rule in the world today.

# FAITHFULNESS:
## 1 Corinthians 4:11, 12

# GOD'S FAITHFUL STEWARDS

Faithfulness is a quality of Christian character and a spiritual value that God desires and expects from all His people. Its expression through faithful behavior is a consequence of personal connectedness and relationship with Jesus. And only through living the life of Christ in us, can we as stewards of the kingdom bear this fruit of faithfulness. In this concept article, I will present two great stewards of the Old Testament and illustrate how their faithfulness as an expression of their stewardship became a blessing to others.

## *Joseph—God's Faithful Steward in Egypt*

A key personal reference with regard to Joseph's early life in Egypt is the phrase "the Lord was with him" (Gen. 39:21), which appears several times in Genesis 39. This notation that "the Lord was with Joseph" (Gen. 39:2, 23) would indicate that God's presence was with him as a young person, even in a foreign land. Whereas he was far away from his family and community, yet he was not out of sight of God's radar of divine grace and sovereignty. And in God's providence, Joseph was placed in Egypt to serve as a savior for his family and a steward of the Lord.

"The Lord was with Joseph" would also mean that God was an integral part of his daily living and experience. This was the case when he was tempted by Potiphar's wife to sleep with her, and he replied, "How then could I do such a wicked thing and sin against God?" (Gen. 39:9). For Joseph, sin was not just about a violation of trust between him and his master or taking advantage of a character weakness in Potiphar's wife, but a serious infringement into his own relationship with God. Every act and decision of his heart was measured in relationship to the will of his God, and in this sense he was a faithful steward.

But the repetitiveness of the phrase "the Lord was with him" (Gen. 39:3, 21) would also imply that God's presence and His centrality in Joseph's life were not an accident but a matter of personal choice. Joseph chose to have God as the center of his universe, and everything else was periphery and secondary to this spiritual value. Joseph's upbringing and home education no doubt played an important part in his faithfulness to God, but with every test he faced he chose to honor God, and God in turn honored him. By putting God first, Joseph experienced prosperity and success; and he found favor in the eyes of Potiphar and the prison warden (Gen. 39:2, 3, 4, 21, 23). Additionally, the Bible noted that Joseph's life as steward brought blessings to "everything Potiphar had both in the house and in the field" (Gen. 39:5).

## *Daniel—God's Faithful Steward in Babylon*

Like Joseph, Daniel was taken out of his homeland and people and was relocated in the courts of the conquering king—Nebuchadnezzar (Dan. 1:1-4). In both cases, however, God as Lord of the universe manifested His presence (Dan. 1:9) and power in miraculous ways, thus overruling earthly situations that would have otherwise brought ultimate destruction and an unexpected end (Dan. 2:12) to these young stewards.

In his very first test (food) as a prisoner of war, Daniel made a brave decision (Dan. 1:8) that demonstrated principle and resilience, which are expressions of Christian stewardship. For Daniel, being removed from his religious community at Palestine was not a reason to compromise his way of life as a Jew or his core beliefs as a follower and worshiper of Yahweh. More important, his decision to honor God by staying with a simple vegetarian diet brought immediate and superior results. "At the end of the ten days they looked healthier and better nourished than any of the young men who ate the royal food" (Dan. 1:15). "In every matter of wisdom and understanding about which the king questioned them, he found them ten times better than all the magicians and enchanters in his whole kingdom" (Dan. 1:20). By putting God first and foremost in his life, Daniel experienced the blessings of the Lord.

The test to eat from the food items served for the king was only the beginning of many tests to follow for Daniel and his friends (Shadrach, Meshach, and Abednego). King Nebuchadnezzar in the second year of his reign had a dream that bothered him much. But while Daniel was not part of the "wise" men of Babylon called to interpret the king's dream, at the end he was certainly counted and included to be executed for the failure of others (Dan. 2:10-13).

Faced with a matter of life and death, Daniel again showed wisdom in handling this delicate situation by speaking first to Arioch with "tact" (Dan. 2:14). Second, he made a personal appearance and appeal to the king for more time. This was a bold move on his part. Third, he, together with his friends, through prayer sought the "God of heaven" for mercy (Dan. 2:18).

Daniel was a strategic thinker, and God rewarded his personal efforts and faith by revealing to him the very same dream that Nebuchadnezzar had. At the end of this challenge the king appointed Daniel to be "ruler over the entire province of Babylon and placed him in charge of all its wise men" (Dan. 2:48). Daniel was God's steward in Babylon. "Moreover, at Daniel's request the king appointed Shadrach, Meshach, and Abednego administrators over the province of Babylon, while Daniel himself remained at the royal court" (Dan. 2:49). It pays to be faithful!

## LOCAL CHURCH STEWARDSHIP:
*Malachi 3:10 (... so much blessing ...)*

# STEWARDSHIP AND THE LOCAL CHURCH

In the structure of the Seventh-day Adventist Church, from the local church all the way to the General Conference, the local church is the most important organizational unit. It's in the local church where Adventist members meet regularly for Christian fellowship, Bible study, prayer, worship, and witness, and where Christian ministry is done. It's in the local church where disciples are made, trained, and nurtured. It's in the local church where rapport with the community is established and bridges of understanding are built. It's in the local church where mission is promoted and members are challenged for service. It's in the local church where offerings are received and tithe is returned; and it's in the local church where stewardship education takes place. In this article, I will share with our leaders key components (education, communication, and offering systems) of our stewardship strategy that are best implemented in the local church setting.

## *Pastors Are Stewardship Educators*

As spiritual leaders for the church, pastors are placed in an ideal situation to influence and challenge church members to a higher level of commitment and connectedness to God. Through their life and ministry, they can model spirituality and mentor church elders toward a life where Jesus is the center. This aspect of spiritual leadership can be done on a one-to-one basis with specific elders or within the context of a small group (elders' council or church board), depending on the size of the church.

Helping members to experience Christ personally cannot be limited to church leaders or to the Sabbath only. In fact, it is a function of leadership that needs to be done daily and across the board for the benefit of the whole congregation. This emphasis on spirituality has to be the foundation for pastoral ministry in the local church, and it must be an integral part of the culture of the congregation. This work of the pastor can be done through home visitation (personal appreciation and encouragement included), preaching (affirmation of members is expressed), teaching (including financial stewardship), chairing of meetings (where the church's vision is refined and promoted), or in the mentoring of others (leaders and members).

## *Wholistic Stewardship Education*

Wholistic stewardship education finds its starting point in God as Creator, Owner, Sustainer, Provider, Savior, and Lord of all. It emphasizes the importance of being in relationship with Jesus, and the willingness of the believer to be in partnership with God. Wholistic stewardship education looks at the totality of our human experience in response to the fullness of God in Christ Jesus. It is the surrendering of the entire life (leadership, relationships, possessions, language, etc.) to the rulership of God in the world, which includes the returning of tithe and the giving of freewill offerings (financial stewardship) in the context of Christian worship. Any other approach that ignores the spiritual dimension of biblical stewardship and focuses only on money (including financial management) is not wholistic and will not be sustainable in the long run. This ongoing work of stewardship education in the local church can be done by the local pastor or by others in conjunction with local conference or union training programs.

## *Communication and Information Strategy*

In addition to the preaching, teaching, and modeling of Christian stewardship, it is also very important that church members are receiving correct and timely information on a regular basis. Such information may include the amounts of tithe and offerings received; how these funds are being used in the work of mission, both locally and globally; and how financial giving is making a difference in the ministry of the church in some specific part of the world. The delivery of accurate and current information builds trust among membership, and it can result in increased commitment by members to the work of God.

How to communicate these kinds of information to members will vary from church to church, but there are some very basic and inexpensive means of communication that can be employed for this purpose. The Sabbath bulletin is one such avenue, and by adding special stewardship inserts or bookmarks with stewardship messages in the bulletin can also maximize the usefulness of this tool. Placing stewardship quotes and current stewardship news items on the projection screen between Sabbath School and the worship service can create interest in stewardship, while providing a critical communication link between members and the church.

Other communication means may include verbal affirmation and expression of appreciation by leaders Sabbath morning, and the presentation of mission and financial reports during board and business meetings of the church.

## *The Offering Systems*

Helping members to understand the particular offering system operating in the local conference and division, whether it is the Calendar of Offerings (COO), Personal Giving Plan (PGP), or the Combined Offerings Plan (COP), is critical to the success of stewardship practice in the local church. Information on any one of these systems is readily available through the local conference; and the local church can also request assistance, if necessary, from the conference treasury for someone to help members understand how the Adventist church supports mission and ministry through offerings.

If the Adventist Church is to succeed in making mature stewards of God's kingdom in the world today, then I challenge all of us who are leaders to prayerfully consider this stewardship strategy as a means of revitalizing Christian stewardship in the local church.

# TITHING:
## *God's Portion*

# IT IS AN ACT OF WORSHIP

The Seventh-day Adventist Church, since its early beginning as a mission movement, recognized the importance of returning tithe, 10 percent of one's increase/income, to God through the local congregation. Initially, this faith practice based on Scripture was seen as necessary in supporting the work of God in the world. As a body of Christian believers, we continue to teach and support this stewardship tradition in the life of the church today. Stewardship is the total response of the Christian steward to God in ALL things, including finances, and tithe and offerings are part of our financial stewardship (Mark 12:30). Whereas there are many and varied perspectives on the subject of tithing, I want to share this understanding from the standpoint of worship.

## *Worship the Creator*

Genesis 14 provides for us the first biblical reference to tithing. "Then Melchizedek king of Salem brought out bread and wine. He was priest of

God Most High, and he blessed Abram, saying, 'Blessed be Abram by God Most High, Creator of heaven and earth. And blessed be God Most High, who delivered your enemies into your hand.' Then Abram gave him a tenth of everything" (Gen. 14:18-20, NIV).

While the setting where Abraham returned tithe was the aftermath of battle (after he defeated Kedorlaomer and his allies), the acknowledgement of God as the "Creator" and the "Most High" by Melchizedek, who was king and priest at the same time, are important to note because these are worship expressions. More important, Abraham's returning of tithe was a worship response to the declaration of who God is. In fact, even with his reply to the king of Sodom, he acknowledged "the Lord, God Most High, Creator of heaven and earth" (Gen. 14:22, NIV). These verbal expressions of worship by Melchizedek and Abraham, I believe, are not accidental mounds in the larger landscape of the Bible, but intentional landmarks reminding people everywhere that God is worthy of praise and worship, and that the returning of tithe is part of a worship experience.

Another significant observation to highlight in the Genesis 14 account on tithe is the fact that Abraham was "blessed" first by Melchizedek before he returned tithe to him (14:19). We return tithe not because of our desire to receive a blessing from God, but because we are blessed already; and we want to acknowledge Him as the sustainer of life and provider of every good gift. Our motive for returning tithe first and foremost is worship; He is the Creator God. I find this perspective on tithing refreshing, biblical, and spiritual. It is not about me; it is about God.

## *Into the Storehouse*

A very important element in the practice of returning tithe to God by the Israelites was the fact that tithes were returned to a central place—the temple, or more specifically, the storerooms at the temple (Neh. 10:37-39). Nehemiah, in addition to reminding the returning Jews of the tithing legislation as set out in the law (and as recorded in the book of Numbers), also established a system where Levites were appointed to bring the tithes from the countryside to the temple storerooms. Interestingly, the people's response to this reestablishment of the rightful place of tithing in their religious life and at the temple was received with this pledge of commitment: "We will not neglect the house of our God" (Neh. 10:39, NIV).

While this promise may, in the first instance, be a reference to their commitment to the temple services, I would suggest that this was also a commitment to worshiping God, who dwells in the temple. The very ritual of returning tithe to the temple was a worship practice. It meant that tithe belongs to God, and that it was to be returned to His place of worship. In essence, tithe and the returning of it to the storerooms was a constant reminder to God's people in the Old Testament to worship Him who made everything. In the Seventh-day Adventist Church, we normally return tithe on Sabbath as part of our worship service.

## A Call to Worship

The message of Malachi is not about tithe and offerings, but about acceptable worship—the total giving of one's self to God (Mal. 3). In Chapter 1, for example, God reminded Israel of the value of respect and honor that He expects and deserves from them (Mal. 1:6). This respect and honor are best expressed in the giving of unblemished animal sacrifices in worship (1:7-10), but Israel instead was giving God the sickly and the rejects of their flocks. In Chapter 2, God called for the whole community to return to Him, and to turn away from their evil ways and idolatry (2:11). He also made clear to Israel the consequences of His judgment if they fail to heed His call and the fact that their offerings will not appease Him (2:12).

God detests superficial and pretense worship (2:13). So in the middle of this call to worship, God reminded Israel of His desire for them to be reconnected to Him (3:6). "Return to me, and I will return to you." When they return to Him, He expects them also to return to Him His tithe and offerings (3:10). Tithe and offerings, His properties, were to be returned as part of their worship experience, and these were to be returned to the "storehouse."

# STEWARD-LEADER:
## *Anointed Appointed*

# STEWARDSHIP AND PASTORAL LEADERSHIP

It is a fact today that most Seventh-day Adventist pastors never had a class or course in stewardship during their ministerial training. At least this was my experience; yet the church expects pastors to promote and teach the local congregation the principles and practices of Christian stewardship. With this reality as a background, I want to offer some suggestions on what pastors can do to grow faithful stewards in their local congregations. To help you understand my perspective in this article, I want to state two assumptions. First, the goal of Christian stewardship is to help individuals connect and have an experience with Jesus Christ as Savior and Lord. Second, the focus of stewardship education is value transformation.

## Preach Biblical Stewardship

Given the role of the pastor as the primary religious educator, and based on my own experience in the local church, I am convinced that preaching Christ (His person, His life, His ministry) with a broad focus on the larger themes of stewardship will change people's hearts, attitudes, and behavior. Preaching the Word is powerful because people accept this as the voice of God speaking through the expository presentation of Scripture. And when Christ is the focus, this moves the center of the universe from self to God; a major paradigm shift for some people and the beginning of a new life and experience with Him. Preach on stewardship at least once a month.

## Teach Financial Stewardship

Whereas preaching may cover a broad range of biblical themes and topics (and sometimes without mentioning the word "stewardship"), teaching financial stewardship has a much narrower focus: tithe and offerings. Teaching financial stewardship is necessary because it provides the pastor or the local stewardship leader the opportunity to address the specifics of returning the Lord's tithe and the giving of freewill offerings. In addition to teaching biblical principles and practices of financial stewardship in the Bible, this is also the right time to help church members understand the church's financial system and how it impacts mission both locally and globally. Opportunity must also be given during these sessions for people to ask questions and share testimonies, and quite often these are invaluable times to clarify issues and affirm their faith in God and the church. I suggest scheduling two teaching sessions on financial stewardship per calendar year.

## Regular Visitation and Affirmation

I recognize that in some situations and parts of the world, visiting people in their homes or offices may not always be possible, but the underlying principle is that connecting with individuals is very important, and it can pay big dividends in terms of human relationships and support for the pastor and the church. Being in touch with people whatever the means opens up lines of communication and better understanding while offering the pastor opportunity to thank church members for their faithfulness to God. One way of affirming members in their stewardship is by thanking the congregation or acknowledging certain individuals during the worship time. Something simple, but it can be very effective and often is better.

## *Report Often*

Church members are not donors, they are stewards; but they would like to know how their giving is making a difference in the life and ministry of the church. Unfortunately, the church is perceived to be quick in asking and reminding people of their financial obligations but very slow in reporting back to its constituents and members. In the local congregation there are a number of time slots and tools to disseminate information: the Sabbath bulletin, announcement time between Sabbath School and the worship service, church board and business meetings. By reporting and sharing information freely and frequently, the pastor can create a culture of trust and transparency within the church as well as biblical values that people are looking for when searching for a church to belong to.

## *Modeling and Mentoring*

Faithfulness as a human behavior is contagious, and it is caught more than taught. I understand that faithfulness as seen on the surface/outside is an expression of Jesus' presence on the inside of us (it is Christ living out His life in me); people also take more notice of what we do than what we say. In the local church, what the pastor does speaks louder than what he or she may say to the congregation. When the pastor is faithful in the returning of tithe and the giving of offerings, the members will follow suit. When members see that their pastor is a good steward with health, leadership, family, time, devotional life, and the management of finances, they will want to behave like him or her.

The point I am making is simple: our members will follow us wherever we lead them; and our personal influence can have an immediate and long-term effect on the way they live their lives and in their service for God. This is a wonderful opportunity to make a difference by simply living the life of a steward, and God's grace is sufficient to help us when we are weak and feel inadequate. But whatever approach you may decide to use to promote and encourage faithfulness in your little corner of the world, what is important is to remember that stewardship is not another program of the church to implement, but a way of life; living for Jesus 24/7.

STEWARDSHIP REVIVAL:
*Reviving Stewardship—Transforming Stewards*

# REVIVING STEWARDSHIP: TRANSFORMING STEWARDS

The call for "revival and reformation" by Pastor Ted Wilson, president of the General Conference of Seventh-day Adventists, is an invitation for the church to renew itself spiritually and to refocus on what is most important in terms of its life and mission. This call to revival assumes that something is already at work, and this something is the working of the Spirit of God in the world and in the lives of people. It also recognizes that the church is continually bombarded by the devil in his attempts to take God's people away from Him. In this context, it is very normal and possible for people to lose their focus on Jesus—the author and finisher of our faith (Heb. 12:1, 2).

# Reviving Stewardship

The call for revival is necessary and needed. At this time God's church is called to look at Jesus anew, and to reach out to Him for His power to both live and do His will. Stewardship, as a ministry of the church, takes this challenge seriously. In this article we will look at these two aspects of "revival" and "reformation" within the framework of stewardship ministries. We will illustrate how stewardship is a ministry "tool" and a partner in this call and invitation for the Seventh-day Adventist Church to be revived and transformed.

# Stewardship—a Spiritual Experience

Many Christians and Seventh-day Adventists think of stewardship as a matter of finances only; meaning, the returning of tithe and the giving of offerings. While finances may be part of stewardship, by themselves they do not reflect the whole picture of stewardship as expressed in the Bible. Stewardship first and foremost is an acknowledgement of who God is—Creator, Owner, Sustainer, Lord, and Savior.

Biblical stewardship is a spiritual experience where one accepts and submits to the rule of God in Jesus Christ (Matt. 6:33). This spiritual experience and relationship with God is primary, and the living out of His rule in one's life is what stewardship is all about. It is a way of life where Jesus is the focus of everything we do: our worship, relationships, possessions, finances, and human expressions.

# Stewardship—a Spiritual Discipline

Stewardship is a personal choice to let Jesus take control of our lives. In this sense it is a spiritual discipline. It calls for our full cooperation and partnership with the Spirit of God working within us. For example, the setting aside of a special time for personal Bible study and prayer is stewardship. The intentional planning of family worship and devotion is stewardship. The scheduling of regular time for physical exercise is stewardship. The systematic returning of tithe and the giving of freewill offerings is stewardship. Personal decisions and choices are part and parcel of stewardship—it is a spiritual response and discipline of the Christian life.

## Transforming Stewards

The goal of Christian stewardship is a valuable transformation at the deepest level of our being where Christ is constantly working within us. This work of changing us from the inside out by the Holy Spirit is a must, because we cannot do this on our own (John 15:4, 5). In fact, it is impossible because of our sinful nature. Our only hope in producing that which is pure and right is through Him working in us and for us (Gal. 2:20). Let me illustrate. It is not our normal self to be kind and forgiving of one another, but rather it is Christ manifesting His life in us. The work of God in us is also shown in relational activities such as our faithful Sabbath attendance and when sharing our faith in Christ. More important, these behavioral changes happen naturally, because they are produced and motivated by the Spirit of God.

## Transformation and Financial Stewardship

If transformation is the work of God, and I believe it is, then how can this behavioral change taking place in my mind and value system impact my faithfulness in returning the Lord's tithe and the giving of freewill offerings? First, faithfulness becomes a way of life. Very often we do it even without thinking about it.

Second, faithfulness flows out of us naturally without coercion or manipulation. It is not dependent upon or motivated by external promotions or rewards. Third, our giving becomes regular, and it includes giving in all other areas of the Christian life: time, spiritual gifts, family, possessions, etc. Fourth, giving becomes a joy. It is no longer an obligation of church membership but an extension and expression of a loving relationship.

Stewardship Ministries is committed to spiritual renewal in the church through its ongoing educational and training activities around the world, while at the same time focusing on Jesus and His Spirit as the transforming power to bring about lasting changes in the lives of God's people everywhere.

# THE SPIRIT OF SACRIFICE:
## *My All in Response to God's All*

# IT'S ABOUT KNOWING GOD

While attending the June 2011 stewardship advisory in the Southern Africa-Indian Ocean Division in Pretoria, South Africa, I was reminded of the sacrifice and commitment made by church workers in Zimbabwe in 2008. For a 12-month period, the Zimbabwe Union Conference was unable to remunerate them for their services because of the impact of inflation on the Zimbabwean economy and the value of the Zimbabwean dollar at the time. With this one example of faithfulness to God in mind, I've asked myself this question: "What makes people such as these workers commit themselves to the cause of God in the face of financial hardship and personal loss?" A selected study on the life of Abraham from the Old Testament may help us gain insight into the dynamics of such deep commitment and personal sacrifice by many Seventh-day Adventists around the world today.

## Giving Up Isaac

Genesis 22 starts with the interesting notation that "God tested Abraham" (vs. 1). This introduction shows that the giving of Isaac as a "sacrifice" was a response to something initiated by God. God wanted to test Abraham's "faith"—his character and behavior—within the context of their relationship. Of this test the author of Hebrews testified, "By faith Abraham, when God tested him, offered Isaac as a sacrifice. He who had received the promises was about to sacrifice his one and only son" (Heb. 11:17, NIV).

The Genesis and Hebrews accounts of this story seem to imply that the testing of one's faith is a necessary challenge and process in one's relationship with God. Writing to the first-century Christians on the subject of trials and the testing of one's faith, James made this assertion: "Consider it pure joy, my brothers, whenever you face trials of many kinds, because you know that the testing of your faith develops perseverance. Perseverance must finish its work so that you may be mature and complete, not lacking anything" (James 1:2-4, NIV).

## Abraham's Spirit of Sacrifice

One other observation that is worth noting with regard to Abraham's spirit of sacrifice as illustrated in this moving story of faith, was the fact that he was obedient to God even to the point of losing his "only son," the most precious and invaluable possession he had received from God. This unbelievable demand from God and Abraham's incredible response can be understood and appreciated fully only when placed within the larger context of his life—a man who had waited for many years to see the fulfillment of God's promise of a descendant that was to come from his own body and to become a blessing for the whole world; but now he had to give it back fully as a sacrifice!

This incident in Abraham's life is a powerful illustration of stewardship coming full circle. That Abraham, in placing his son Isaac on the altar as a sacrifice, was simply returning to God His gift. God is the rightful owner and original giver of Isaac, Abraham's son. This act of sacrificial giving would suggest to me that when God calls for a sacrifice from us, His people, He will not settle for anything less than our very best. He wants that thing that is very close to our hearts. Stewardship is about giving our all.

## *Trusting in the Ultimate Giver and Provider*

Another overriding and fundamental principle in this Bible example of sacrifice and commitment is the truth that God is our provider; and that He will always deliver even if we can't see the end from the beginning. This kind of trust—in a believable end in the absence of any physical evidence—is still difficult, and so when Isaac posed an innocent but rational question from his position as a "son" and partner in this whole faith-testing experience with God, it must have crushed Abraham's heart. "The fire and wood are here," Isaac said, "but where is the lamb for the burnt offering?" (Gen. 22:7, NIV). From his vantage point as a father and a human being, Abraham could see only Isaac; he was the offering "lamb." And yet from his heart of hearts he believed God. And so in spite of his agonizing and aching heart, Abraham never wavered in his response, "God Himself will provide" (Gen. 22:7, 8, NIV).

Stewardship is about absolute trust in God. How shall we answer the following question: "What made Abraham do what he did when he placed Isaac on the altar as a sacrifice to God?" I believe the answer has to do with Abraham's intimate relationship with God. He knew Him as a personal friend, and the giving of Isaac as a sacrifice was a physical expression of a deep and close relationship with God. Paul the apostle puts it this way; "He believed God, and it was credited to him as righteousness" (Gal. 3:6, NIV).

Abraham may not have seen the end from the beginning, but he knew God and he trusted Him.

For Seventh-day Adventist Christians in Zimbabwe; for the early pioneers of our faith, people such as James and Ellen White and John Andrews; for Abraham of the Bible; and for most believers around the world, their motive for giving their all and sacrificing much for the mission of God in this world is rooted in their personal relationship with Him. They know God as the Owner, the ultimate Giver, and Provider of life. For them, commitment and sacrifice are normal ways of living.

## WHOLE LIFE OFFERING:
*Are You a Cheerful Giver?*

# OFFERINGS: IT'S ALL ABOUT THANKSGIVING

Whereas believers return tithe to God as an expression of their faithfulness to Him, offerings are given as acts of gratitude for what God has done for His people. It's about acknowledging His blessings. It's about our willingness to recognize God as the Creator, Owner, and Giver of every good and perfect gift (James 1:17). As Seventh-day Adventists, we return tithe and give offerings as part of our financial stewardship to God. Very often this is done in the context of our weekly worship time, when we join fellow believers each Sabbath at our local congregations. In this article, I want to help clarify our understanding of offerings and our giving practices as Adventists.

### *Give and Let God*

Tithe and offerings are distinct in nature but work in a similar way. Offerings, like tithe, become God's the very moment the decision has been made in the individual's heart to give the offering, whether by percentage of income or an actual amount. Once offerings are thus assigned to God, the ownership is transferred to Him and they no longer belong to us. They have become God's property. Once the ownership of the gift is released and transferred from me to God, the offerings become "holy." This money is now set aside for God's purposes. It will be used in support of His mission and the ministries of His church, both locally and globally. But unlike tithe, where God has already set the percentage, i.e., 10 percent to be returned to Him, offerings are left to the believers' discretion. It's a matter of the heart. It's a voluntary and free expression of the human will and generosity. This is a key difference between tithe and offerings. The amount of giving in offerings is not mandated, stipulated, or legislated. An offering is something that every believer must decide on within their own heart well before the Sabbath begins.

## *The Measure of Giving*

In the giving of offerings, God grants us the privilege of choosing how best to give a gift that represents our heartfelt gratitude for what He has done and who He is. While the actual amount of money or the percentage of our giving is ours to decide, God nevertheless expects that we give Him our best! When the Israelites failed to give God what He was due, He chastised them: "Cursed is the cheat who has an acceptable male in his flock and vows to give it, but then sacrifices a blemished animal to the Lord" (Mal. 1:14).

In the Scriptures, there are two principles that can assist us in the matter of freewill giving. First, we give our offerings to God on the basis of His blessings upon us (Deut. 16:17). What we give is "in proportion" to what we have received from Him. Second, we give to God from a grateful heart (2 Cor. 8:12; 9:7). When giving an offering, the motive for giving and the condition of the heart are just as important as the gift itself. For example, Jesus measured the worth of the widow's offerings not according to what she gave, but rather on what was left after she gave it (Luke 21:4). Heaven does not determine the value of an offering by comparing it with the amounts given by others. Rather, God sees the value in the personal sacrifice and the heart's commitment that prompt the giving. This does not mean that freewill giving is a license to give nothing. It is the choice we have as stewards to give our best to God—over and beyond what has already been returned in tithe.

# *Systematic Giving*

As Adventists, we've encouraged our members through stewardship education to return the Lord's tithe and give Him our offerings of thanksgiving systematically. Here are seven important pointers that can help us make our giving more systematic, sacrificial, and spontaneous in the context of worship, while at the same time supporting God's mission to make disciples of all peoples:

1. Because financial giving is an act of worship and a way of life, we are to give careful thought and planning during the week as to what we will give to God on Sabbath. Giving should include advance planning with the whole family.

2. Good financial stewardship begins with the systematic returning of the Lord's tithe. God is the absolute owner of everything. We are to put aside this portion of His blessings from our income first.

3. In addition to tithe, we are to put aside our regular offerings of thanksgiving. These offerings may go toward the local church budget and/or other ministry needs of the church beyond the local congregation.

4. Systematic giving also makes provision for additional offerings to be given for special projects and to the needs of the poor in society. It should be noted, however, that giving to special projects is not a substitute for regular offerings or the Lord's tithe.

5. In systematic giving, Adventists are reminded of the needs of God's mission across the globe and at home. This principle of giving to both the local and global church is a unique feature of Adventist giving, which applies to both tithe and offerings.

6. Systematic giving is regular giving.

7. Systematic giving helps us, individually and corporately, to focus on God and mission.

The Seventh-day Adventist Church is where it is today in terms of its growth and ministry because of the blessings of God and the faithfulness of its members across the globe. As director for Stewardship Ministries of the General

Conference, I am grateful that God's people show such faithfulness in returning the Lord's tithe and giving offerings of thanksgiving to Him. We love Him because He first loved us (1 John 4:19), and giving is all about a thankful heart.

# THE GIFT OF TIME:
## *What Am I Doing With His Time?*

# ALL FOR JESUS

Celebrating the life of a loved one in death . . . it seemed such a contradiction. It was only a few days into the New Year (2012), and here we all were in church, where I, as a pastor and friend of the family, was invited to present an appropriate message of hope and encouragement to all in attendance. Many members of the extended family were not Seventh-day Adventist Christians.

The deceased, a mother, grandmother, and great-grandmother, had lived for more than 93 years and passed away only a few months before she turned 94. I began the eulogy by reading this verse from the Scriptures: "Our days may come to seventy years, or eighty, if our strength endures; yet the best of them are but trouble and sorrow, for they quickly pass, and we fly away" (Ps. 90:10, NIV). Here was my point: "She lived her life to the full, and she gave all of her life (time) to God." As Christian stewards, we recognize that time is a gift of God, and that we are charged with the sacred responsibility of living it and using all of it for His glory (1 Cor. 10:3).

## Time of Birth

In my family, we celebrate our children's birthdays in November (Janae-Grace) and December (Jaydon), and it is our family custom on these special occasions to first acknowledge God as the giver of life. We do this during our family worship time, but we also put money aside as an offering of thanksgiving to be given on the following Sabbath, in recognition of God's sustenance and the blessings of good health. While this idea of remembering God during birthday times may be obvious for most Christians, it is nevertheless important that we restate this Christian understanding in today's materialistic world. We need to constantly remind ourselves of this biblical fact: it is God who gives life (Gen. 1:1).

Job, a worshiper of Yahweh, in his time of trial and loss, recognized the sovereignty of God and His ownership of everything by declaring, "Naked I came from my mother's womb, and naked I will depart. The Lord gave and the Lord has taken away; may the name of the Lord be praised" (Job 1:21, NIV). Notwithstanding the context of Job being a very rich man, his testimony highlights a fundamental principle of stewardship: God owns everything, including life. Moreover, from the day we are born, there is nothing we receive or possess that belongs to us. Everything we are and have in this world is God's. Time, whether it is measured in seconds or years, is a gift of the Creator God.

## Time for Living

By accepting time as God's gift, we also accept our God-given responsibility, the stewardship of time, which implies good time management. This emphasis on the use of time as a spiritual discipline of the Christian life is powerfully presented by Solomon the "preacher" in this way: "Whatever your hand finds to do, do it with all your might, for in the realm of the dead, where you are going, there is neither working nor planning nor knowledge nor wisdom" (Eccl. 9:10, NIV). The point of this biblical passage is clear. Because this life is finite and brief, we humans and people of God must, therefore, take advantage of every moment we have in life to do all that we can before we die (Eccl. 11:9). However, our personal "doing" and living over time must be informed by the rule of Jesus Christ—the awareness that we live for Him, and in the presence of God.

The question that follows is, "How does this message of maximizing time translate into ways of actually living today?" For me, it means appropriating and spending more time with my family—my wife, Maxine, and my two children. As a PK (pastor's kid), I am very aware of how pastors can become so committed to, and involved in, their ministry that there's very little time left to spend with their immediate families. Setting time aside on a daily basis for our family is good stewardship.

## *Time and Death*

The apostle Paul, toward the end of his life and ministry, made this wonderful conclusive statement: "For to me, to live is Christ and to die is gain" (Phil. 1:21, NIV). When looking at these words in the context of his life and the time he gave freely to the service of God, Paul seems to be saying that there's no other purpose for living except to live for Jesus Christ; and even in the matter of death he considers that too a "gain" because of Christ. For Paul, life finds its true meaning in Christ—the Way, the Truth, and the Life. And it is this unfaltering faith in God's leading in his life—all of the time—that gave Paul the courage to face suffering and death without fear. The basis for such confidence is Christ Himself, who has conquered death and the grave (Rev. 1:17, 18).

To the New Testament church at Smyrna, Jesus said, "Do not be afraid of what you are about to suffer. I tell you, the devil will put some of you in prison to test you, and you will suffer persecution for ten days. Be faithful, even to the point of death, and I will give you life as your victor's crown" (Rev. 2:10, NIV). The call to be faithful to God to the very end of time or to the point of death still holds true for Christian stewards today. Following Jesus as Savior and Lord from birth to death is a lifetime calling. It is a total commitment of heart and life, 24/7. It's all for Jesus. And when He comes, will He find us faithful stewards?

# TALENTED BY GOD:
*What Is Your Influence?*

# TALENTS—GOD'S GIFTS

"She was a true original and a talent beyond compare" (CNN Online News, February 11). This was Quincy Jones's (American music producer) reaction to the sudden and unexpected death (accidental drowning) of Whitney Houston (a legendary pop singer) on Saturday, February 11, 2012. Another great American singer and songwriter, Lionel Richie, told CNN that Whitney "had a voice that could just turn on a story, a melody into magical notes."

Reverend DeForest B. Soaries Jr, senior pastor at First Baptist Church of Lincoln Gardens in Somerset, New Jersey, and a friend of Whitney, remembered her rehearsal with a choir back in 1977 when Whitney was only 14. He said, "This child had invoked a level of divine inspiration that involved the kind of joyous tears and emotional shouts that were characteristics of the black religious experience. Not only did Whitney's singing completely transform the atmosphere, but it was clear to everyone in that rehearsal that they were in the presence of an unusual talent and that they were eyewitness to a superstar taxiing on the runway of success and fame" (CNN Opinion: "The Whitney Houston I Knew," February 13).

Whitney Houston had an angelic voice and a "talent beyond compare," but what is a talent? A talent is a natural and unique ability instilled into one's being by God in His act of creation. This deed of sharing something of Himself with us is expressed well in the Genesis account: "So God created mankind in his own image, in the image of God he created them; male and female he created them" (Gen. 1:27, NIV).

Talents come to us as a gift of His grace at birth, and every human person (Christian or non-Christian) born into this world is endowed with a set of special skills and abilities. For Christians, however, these manifestations of God's creativity and love are given so we can serve and minister to people everywhere while giving Him, our Creator and Maker, the glory (1 Cor. 10:31).

Can talents be refined, improved, and developed to extraordinary quality over time? The answer is yes, and the singing voice of Whitney was a powerful example of a talent that was trained and coached well. Clive Davis, music producer and Whitney's mentor for more than 25 years, noted, "I saw a depth and a range and soul ... that rarely ranks at the top level. And that's why we've been working together ever since" (Davis on CNN's *Piers Morgan Tonight*, February 9, 2012). But as pointed out earlier, a talent is, first and foremost, a God-given ability; and it is given to a person as a "perfect" gift of the Creator (James 1:17). On its own, any talent is extraordinary; and when used and applied at any given time in one's life, it comes across as a "natural" and normal part of their being. Nevertheless, every talent, like any human skill, has the potential for further refinement and improvement. This aspect of development and management is an expression of Christian stewardship.

Can a talent lose its shine, effectiveness, and intended impact? Unfortunately, the answer is also a yes. For Whitney, her smoking and use of drugs affected her ability to reach those high notes that used to make her voice one-of-a-kind. The standard of excellence that she set herself in her rendition of the national anthem at the 1991 Super Bowl, or the soundtrack hit "I Will Always Love You" from the movie *The Bodyguard* (1992), was no longer there when she embarked on a comeback Australian tour in February 2010. Her once clean image of a girl with a pristine voice was now tarnished because of an undesirable lifestyle. Perhaps a lesson that we can all learn from the sad ending of Whitney's life is that we, as followers of Christ, need to value and take care of our God-given talents.

Can a talent be a "spiritual gift" as well? Absolutely! In terms of one's "gift mix," all gifts (talents, acquired skills, and spiritual gifts) come from God, and as such it is possible that a talent may be used by God in a given time and place to complement the needs of ministry. But unlike spiritual gifts, which are received as part of the blessings of conversion, talents are received at the time of one's natural birth. While a talent (e.g., a voice for singing) may stay with a person for life, their spiritual gifts may vary from time to time and given as additional skills for a specific purpose and service. The end purpose for both talents and spiritual gifts, however, is meant to be the same: to minister to others and to bring glory to God.

As Christian stewards, we recognize that life and giftedness, as expressed in people's natural abilities, acquired skills, and spiritual gifts, are measures of God's grace given freely because of His unconditional love and mercies. As gifts of grace they are not given for self-exaltation or personal praise, but granted to us to be used in service to humanity and in extending the boundaries of God's kingdom on earth. Along with the privilege of receiving these gifts comes the responsibility of developing them to the full, and using them in the process of making disciples, while giving glory to Him who is worthy of our praise. But when we fail to use our talents, or when we abuse or misuse these blessings, we can lose them forever.

# CALLED TO SERVE:
*Go Light Your World!*

# SERVICE IS HEART COMMITMENT

I had just returned from Reykjavik, Iceland, after attending the Trans-European Division Stewardship Advisory. I had chosen to fly with Icelandair, the Icelandic airline, on this trip. A few days later I received an e-mail message from the airline inviting my participation in their service survey. The purpose of the survey is to discover ways of improving both the quality of service and the products offered to their passengers, in order to maintain and increase the loyalty of passengers to their airline. Airlines such as this recognize that they exist to offer quality service and vie to better what other airlines may offer for the routes that they service. Indeed, the profitability of the company is dependent to a large extent upon their ability to offer the best service and products in their particular market niche. Service is the difference between a successful and profitable airline and a bankrupt, failed company.

## Service and Quality

But what does service have to do with Christian stewardship? Everything! Both Christian stewardship and service begin with a theological understanding of Creation. True service is an awareness that I, as a created human being, was made after the "image" of the Creator God (Gen. 1:27) and that God makes everything beautiful (Ps. 139:13, 14). Service is an innate response to the invitation of God to extend His rule, creativity, and quality of workmanship to everything we are and do in this world (Gen. 1:28). As Christian stewards, God expects us to demonstrate and express this by the way we live. In doing so we will reflect in our daily lives His creatorship and His standard of being. The awareness of the briefness of life and the certainty of death brought the wise man in the wisdom literature to this conclusion: "Whatever your hand finds to do, do it with all your might" (Eccl. 9:10). The ultimate standard and goal for living is to bring glory to God (1 Cor. 10:31). In the corporate church, service may also mean our ability to represent God accurately by delivering top ministry products to the world in which we live.

## Service and Witness

As in the instance of Icelandair, service is a call to stakeholders (members and employees) in the company to be committed to the mission of the organization. As Seventh-day Adventists, our mission is to make disciples for Jesus Christ in this world, and to help people experience Him as their Savior and Lord. This call to be partners with God in mission includes living as faithful followers of Jesus in the home, the marketplace, and the community. Jesus sums up this call with the following challenge to His disciples: "But you will receive power when the Holy Spirit comes on you; and you will be my witnesses in Jerusalem, and in all Judea and Samaria, and to the ends of the earth" (Acts 1:8). Witness is a person, not a program.

## Service and Worship

In the Sermon on the Mount (Matt. 5-7), Jesus called His disciples and the multitude to worship the Creator God by saying, "No one can serve two masters. Either you will hate the one and love the other, or you will be devoted to the one and despise the other. You cannot serve both God and money" (Matt.

6:24). While the illustration used here was financial wealth (actual money), Jesus was in fact calling His followers to a higher plane of living—it's called worship. It is the kind of worship that focuses on the Giver, and not the gifts; a worship that dwells on eternal values and not on temporal benefits. The kind of worship advocated by Jesus is God-centered and not works-oriented. This is the worship and service that is acceptable to God.

In Revelation 14:7 the first of three angels delivers an urgent cry for the times in which we live, answering questions to do with the elements of worship, service, and stewardship: "Fear God and give him glory, because the hour of his judgment has come. Worship him who made the heavens, the earth, the sea and the springs of water."

# GOD'S TREASURY:
## *Great Is Thy Faithfulness*

# SOVEREIGN AND OWNER OF ALL

Everything in this world belongs to God. This is an undeniable fact of Scripture: "In the beginning God created the heavens and the earth" (Gen. 1:1, NIV). To ensure that this biblical fact is not lost to the reader, the author of Genesis repeated and restated the same message in this way: "This is the account of the heavens and the earth when they were created, when the Lord God made the earth and the heavens" (Gen. 2:4, NIV). God, sovereign Lord of the universe, is owner of everything on this planet on the basis of His creation of it. As Creator, He owns all.

While this understanding of biblical truth is fundamental to the Christian faith, it took personal experience to drive this point home for me. Let me illustrate this. It was the most wonderful experience being with my wife when she gave birth to our two children. Each time I marveled at creation and the powerful demonstration of God's amazing grace and His power to sustain human life in the womb, right up to that point when the newborn baby takes up life on its own away from the mother, and then further. Here then is the biblical truth and stewardship principle that I learned from those two occasions. As humans, we enter this world with absolutely nothing. No clothes, no toys, no money, not anything.

## *God Is Sovereign Owner*

The story of Job testifies to God's ownership of all in a most dramatic way. Job was a very wealthy person with a large household (Job 1:2, 3). He had ten children at the beginning of the story. Most important, Job feared God and lived a blameless life. In spite of his personal relationship with God, however, Job lost almost everything in one day, except for his wife and his own life (Job 1:13-19). I've experienced the loss of my parents, and that was painful. But Job lost all ten of his children at one time. This traumatic experience would have hit him very hard both physically and emotionally. The Bible tells us that Job tore his clothes, shaved his head, and fell to the ground (Job 1:20)—a sign of a man in great sorrow.

Given the enormity of his personal loss, both in human life and in material possessions, one would expect that Job would have cursed God and given up his faith in Him, but this was not the case. Instead, Job made a spiritual declaration that showed the depth of his understanding and appreciation of God and life. He said, "Naked I came from my mother's womb, and naked I will depart. The Lord gave and the Lord has taken away; may the name of the Lord be praised" (Job 1:21, NIV). By using the imagery of his own birth, Job made the point that humans own nothing in this world, and when we die, we keep nothing. God is owner of everything.

## *Success and Safety Are From the Lord*

An interesting and important detail of this Bible account is the involvement of Satan in human life; and in the case of Job it was direct and personal. Targeting the integrity of Job, Satan accused God of His care and provisions for Job and his family, implying that this was the reason for Job's faith. "Have you not put a hedge around him and his household and everything he has? You have blessed the work of his hands, so that his flocks and herds are spread throughout the land" (Job 1:10, NIV).

While Satan is a liar by nature, on this occasion he spoke the truth, because it was God who blessed Job with everything he had. It was God who had protected Job and his family. It was God who had prospered Job. As Lord of the universe, there was no part of Job's existence and experience that didn't come under the control of the Creator God. He is the source of all blessings.

The fact is that God is still in control of the affairs of His people, even today. Moreover, it is God who has blessed our every human endeavor, including our families, our business initiatives, our possessions, and our material wealth. The question is whether we understand the blessings of life as Job did. Does the way we relate to our families, to our possessions, and to those around us give us away as unaware of who God is, or does it bear testimony to our God—Creator and owner of all?

# THE MARKETPLACE:
## *Conducting God's Business*

# SALT AND YEAST FOR GOD'S KINGDOM

Christ's mandate for His followers to make disciples (Matt. 28:18-20) is a call to us—the church—to live out the Christian life "in" community, and never in isolation from the people of the world. This understanding of the gospel commission was clearly demonstrated in the lifestyle of the early Christian believers who were intentional in establishing good relationships with their neighbors and communities (Acts 2:47). These men and women understood the words of Jesus well when He said they needed to be "salt" and "yeast" in the world.

## *Salt of the Earth*

"You are the salt of the earth. But if the salt loses its saltiness, how can it be made salty again? It is no longer good for anything, except to be thrown out and trampled underfoot" (Matt. 5:13, NIV). With this metaphor, Jesus masterfully highlighted the subtle but powerful effect of salt in everyday living and especially when used in food. I remember in my childhood, living in Samoa, the way we used salt to mask the sourness of unripe mangoes when we decided to eat them green. Salt in those situations changed the taste of an unwanted sour mango to something delicious and appealing for eating. The call by Christ for His immediate followers, the twelve disciples, to be the "salt of the earth" was a challenge for them to be a force for good in the world. The call implied that following Him is not a passive, uneventful experience, but an intentional, active choice to live out the Christian life as a positive influence in human communities. It also implies that choosing to be a disciple of Christ means that we have something important to contribute, i.e., Jesus, and that we're willing to share Him with the world through our active engagement with others. This is stewardship in action.

## *Yeast of the Kingdom*

"He told them still another parable: 'The kingdom of heaven is like yeast that a woman took and mixed into about sixty pounds of flour until it worked all through the dough' " (Matt. 13:33, NIV). On the surface, this parable of Jesus may look contradictory because of the imagery used—the yeast—which in other parts of the Bible is used as a symbol of sin and evil (Mark 8:5). But when taken in this context, which includes the parable of the mustard seed (Matt. 13:31, 32), the message and meaning of the yeast here becomes clear. Like yeast in the dough, God's kingdom brings about growth and change, and we know that this effect is the work of God Himself in us. This change does not take place in a vacuum, however. It happens through the lives of God's people in community with others. By living as faithful stewards and disciples in the marketplace of life, we become transforming agents of God's kingdom. More important, when God acts and He initiates change, His power can be felt and experienced even in the most secular human society.

## *Waiting With Dividends*

In response to the questions asked by His disciples about the end of the world and His second coming (Matt. 24:3), Jesus told them the parable of the "talents," or money. While the primary message remains the same, i.e., that Jesus is coming again, there is also a secondary message and application with regard to financial stewardship in the marketplace. It suggests that it is OK for Christians to wisely and prudently apply their investment skills in the business sector of this world. It is all right to be out there in Wall Street, all the while also being the salt and yeast in the mix, which may result in the changing of someone's life and moving them toward Christ. The call to be a disciple of Jesus is a gospel mandate to be a faithful steward in any of life's vocations, and at all times and in all places; and that our hope and waiting for the return of the Owner must not be an excuse to disengage ourselves from the general populace and human society. In the broad view of Christian stewardship, waiting for Jesus' return means that we will be working faithfully for Him until He comes.

# STEWARDS OF THE EARTH:
## *Our Dominion—God's Domain*

# "AND GOD SAW THAT IT WAS GOOD"

In the beginning God made everything beautiful. The universe, the earth, the trees, and animals of all sizes and colors including birds and butterflies were wonderfully made. Of this creation, the Bible declares that "God saw that it was good" (Gen. 1:4,10).

David, the psalmist, who experienced the awe of the majesty and glory of God in nature, testified of this reality in the following way:

"The heavens declare the glory of God; the skies proclaim the work of his hands. Day after day they pour forth speech; night after night they display knowledge. There is no speech or language where their voice is not heard. Their voice goes out into all the earth, their words to the ends of the world. In the heavens he has pitched a tent for the sun, which is like a bridegroom coming forth from his pavilion, like a champion rejoicing to run his course. It rises at one end of the heavens and makes its circuit to the other; nothing is hidden from its heat" (Ps. 19:1-6; NIV).

While it is true that God's creation in our world today is marred and affected by sin, nature still speaks of the wisdom and power of God as Creator. It is a statement of fact that nature, with all of its unique design, was created for the glory of the Maker and for our enjoyment. In this sense, we see an expression of God's love and care in the natural environment that surrounds us daily. This is a general revelation of God. It makes the statement that He is both Creator and owner of everything.

## *Volcanoes and Vegetation Are Good*

In a visit to Iceland for the Trans-European advisory for treasurers, stewardship ministries, and trust services directors in 2012, my spirit was moved as I looked out on the vast open spaces and contrasting landscapes displaying fresh remains of volcanic activity. In fact, there were still tremors and small earthquakes being registered many miles below ground while we were there. Even today the possibility of future volcanic eruptions is very real. And yet, above ground on this active volcanic landmass one can see green ground cover spotted with colorful wild flowers, gentle thermal streams, snow and ice, and picturesque waterfalls. In many ways I felt as if I were experiencing firsthand the creative acts of God. These were the expressions of God's mind and grace. As a steward, I can only say that "God made all these things beautiful." He saw that this land was good.

## *Waterfalls and Rainbows Are Good*

While visiting our church members and the local congregation near Victoria Falls, on the border of Zimbabwe and Zambia, in May 2012, I was privileged to hear and see the largest curtain of water in the world thundering down the gorge. What amazed me about this wonder of nature was the volume and the power of the water as it rushes through this part of the Zambezi River and down into the gorge. It was an incredible scene to behold. As a matter of fact, we heard the deafening roar of the water crashing down the falls many meters away, long before we were able to see the falls. At about the same time, we also experienced a cool and refreshing shower from the mist generated by the falls carried on the breeze coming from the direction of the Zambezi Gorge. This was a moment to savor and remember. As I was clicking away on the camera, trying to capture this amazing display of water power, there, right above the falls, was another expression of God's presence and promise—a rainbow in the mist. In the language of the Bible, "God saw that it was good."

## *Rainforests and Sand Dunes Are Good*

And so as I reflect on these varied scenes and sounds, not to mention those also of the Amazon rainforest of South America and the sand dunes of the United Arab Emirates in Dubai, I'm just in awe of this great Master Designer who made all these things so different and yet so beautiful. At the same time, I am also reminded, and indeed challenged, that as a Christian steward I'm called to protect and care for these natural resources of the earth for the benefit and enjoyment of others to follow. This is a critical aspect of biblical stewardship.

# STEWARDS OF HOPE:
## *Jesus Is Our Hope*

# JESUS OUR HOPE

I was returning home to the United States from Bangkok, Thailand, in May 2013, after a successful stewardship convention for the Southern Asia-Pacific Division. Yet on this long flight back to Washington, D.C., my heart was aching. I had just lost my first sibling, my brother Enesi to cancer. He lived in New Zealand, and I was away when he died. But somehow in my tired and heartbroken state, these words of Edward Mote (1797–1874) in song came to me as a revelation of God's grace: "My hope is built on nothing less than Jesus' blood and righteousness, / When darkness seems to veil His face, I rest on His unchanging grace; / When all around my soul gives way, He then is all my hope and stay; / On Christ the solid rock I stand; all other ground is sinking sand." In my Christian context, hope cannot be isolated from Jesus Christ, and it cannot exist without His presence. Let me illustrate this thought by reflecting on the experience of Jesus' disciples on that Thursday night, the night just prior to His death on the dark and gloomy Friday afternoon.

## Hope in the Midst of Hopelessness

Hopelessness is living life without the presence of Jesus Christ. After He had washed and dried their feet, and after they had shared bread together, Jesus spoke words of assurance to His disciples. These words cut like a razor into the very core of their being. "My children, I will be with you only a little longer. You will look for me, and just as I told the Jews, so I tell you now: Where I am going, you cannot come" (John 13:33, NIV). For this group of young men, this was a setback. For three years they had waited with anticipation that He, their leader, would establish a new world order that would rescue them from Roman domination. This was an overwhelming disappointment.

How could He do this to them? Where would they go now? To these and other questions spinning around in their heads, Jesus responded, "Do not let your hearts be troubled. You believe in God; believe also in me" (John 14:1, NIV). Jesus' answer to His disciples' sense of hopelessness and loss brought them assurance of His eternal presence. In our world today, where we're constantly faced with all kinds of trials, challenges, human disappointments, emptiness, and hopelessness, Jesus is the answer. Jesus' presence brings encouragement, meaning, value, contentment, certainty, security, and hope. It is this Jesus who has the capacity to calm any of life's storms, bring comfort to the bereaved, and hope to the forsaken and despised of society.

## Christ Is Present Through His Spirit

Recognizing His human limitations to be physically present everywhere, Jesus introduced His disciples to the concept of His omnipresence through the Holy Spirit. "And I will ask the Father, and He will give you another advocate to help you and be with you forever—the Spirit of truth. The world cannot accept Him, because it neither sees Him nor knows Him. But you know Him, for He lives with you and will be in you. I will not leave you as orphans; I will come to you" (John 14:16-18, NIV). To the twelve disciples, these words of their Master lifted their spirits from the depths of hopelessness to new heights riding on His promise and personal assurance. So while He would not be physically available for them, through His Sprit they could experience His presence as a present reality. Today, God's Spirit still fills the void in His disciples' empty and lonely hearts. God's Spirit can turn the nights of darkness into mornings of joy. This presence of Christ in us—through His Spirit—gives us hope both in the here and now and also in the future.

## *God's Peace in the Present*

Whether they recognized it or not, the disciples needed something permanent to satisfy their yearning for companionship and community. And again, Jesus came to them with these comforting words: "But the Advocate, the Holy Spirit, whom the Father will send in my name, will teach you all things and will remind you of everything I have said to you. Peace I leave with you; my peace I give you. I do not give to you as the world gives. Do not let your hearts be troubled and do not be afraid" (John 14:26, 27, NIV).

As Christian stewards, we know that only Jesus can satisfy the desires of our hearts and breathe hope into our own questionings. More important, He expects us, as His followers, to consistently live out this hope by sharing our hope in Him with everyone we meet.

# STEWARDS OF GOD'S TEMPLE:
*My All For His Glory!!!!*

# GOD'S GIFT OF GOOD HEALTH

I'm writing this article on Thanksgiving Day here in Maryland, and my heart is full of praise and gratitude to God for His wonderful gifts of life and good health. Yes, I get sick, and I'm fighting a cold right now; and yes, I get tired; and yes, I'm probably a few pounds heavier than I should be for my height. But despite all of these, I'm still able to do the things I want to do with my family and at work, and I'm thankful to God for the ability to think and move around freely. My body and my health are blessings from above.

## *Stewardship and Christ's Rule*

As I write, I'm also thinking of my grandfather, Puni Ierome, a Samoan chief and orator who lived life to the full until he died in his sleep one Sabbath morning in 1967. He was 106 years of age. Up until the time of his death, he was still able to read his Bible and could engage anyone in conversation without losing his focus. His life was an example and a testimony to what can happen when people make it a priority to take care of their bodies and minds, and follow a few basic principles for healthful living. This is biblical stewardship—living life under the rule of Jesus Christ, and honoring God in the way we live and do things in the world (Rev. 14:6, 7; Rom. 12:1, 2).

## *Health Is a Spiritual Discipline*

I would be the first to admit that my grandfather was not perfect, and he had his own challenges with health and life during his lifetime. He did get sick at times. But he also lived longer than many of his contemporaries, partly owing to his Christian faith and the lifestyle he followed after becoming an Adventist believer. Health for Puni Ierome was a spiritual discipline. It was more than not eating pork or abstaining from alcohol. It was a life that was constantly submitted to the will of God. I know this to be true because I spent the last four years of his life with him.

## *Balance Is Key*

While Adventism meant a total change in lifestyle for Puni Ierome and his family, it was the emphasis on balanced living that he valued. He knew that there was a close relationship between eating right and longevity, and he understood the importance of rest—including cessation from the mundane activities of the first six days of the week in order to worship God on the seventh day, the Sabbath. He was fully aware of the benefits of exercise and physical labor as he worked the fields early in the morning, rested in the afternoon when the sun was too hot for comfort, and went fishing in the evening. He didn't have a motor vehicle, so he walked everywhere. If his fellow villagers or extended family were to go on special long-distance trips along the coast, they would travel as a community in longboats. When it came to nutrition in the village, fresh tropical fruits and vegetables were plentiful in the gardens, and there was an abundance of good drinking water for the family.

# *Social Health in Community*

There are two other invaluable elements in healthful living that I believe contributed to my grandfather's longevity: alertness and peaceful demeanor—right to the end. These qualities were nurtured in the context of social relationships and human interactions.

Building rapport and good relationships with people, both within one's own family and the larger community, as well as in the church, can have positive effects on one's well-being and overall health. And while it is impossible to be stress-free in this world, we're strongly counseled as Christians to love one another and to live in peace with all people (Heb. 12:14; Rom. 13:8). Stewardship is about making the right decisions early in life, and creating an environment where people can live together to accomplish God's purposes in the world.

# STEWARDS OF GOD'S GENEROSITY:
## *More Than Enough*

# GENEROSITY—GOD'S GRACE IN US

Mark Zuckerberg, the founder of Facebook, and his wife, Priscilla Chan, gave a donation of US$970 million last year to the Silicon Valley Foundation, a charity that manages and distributes charitable funds. According to CNNMoney (Melanie Hicken, February 10, 2014), this gift made the couple the top U.S. philanthropists for 2013. Their giving outstripped Bill and Melinda Gates, who gave their foundation slightly over US$181.3 million last year. *The Chronicle of Philanthropy* also reported that Zuckerberg and his wife were the youngest donors on the *The Chronicle*'s list, which has a median age of 72. Why are these people so generous? "*The Chronicle* credits last year's improving economy and booming stock market for the surge in donations" (Hicken, February 10). In short, these billionaires have wealth, and they gave of their riches.

A "nice lady," according to *USA Today* (Melanie Eversley, February 4, 2014), walked into the Boone County Restaurant in Caledonia, Illinois, and tipped three waitresses US$5,000 each. Amay Sabani, 25; Sarah Sckinger, 23; and Amber Kariolich, were organizing silverware and talking about student loans and their dreams of finishing school when their diner and benefactor asked for their names and started writing the checks. Sabani apparently tried to return her check when she saw the amount, but the generous woman refused to take it back. "I want you to take these to help with school and everything else in life. God sent me here to help you." If we take the woman's words at face value, she gave in response to God's prompting. As such, she was an example of God's grace in humankind.

There's another story to tell about generosity, but this time it's from the Bible (2 Cor. 8). This is the testimony of the Macedonian churches. They were extremely poor, but they demonstrated the riches of God's grace in their lives through their extraordinary giving. I would like to highlight three important observations about this group of Christian believers, and their giving.

## *Poor But Generous*

In writing to the Christians at Corinth, the apostle Paul compliments the "rich generosity" of the Macedonian Christians. Unlike the Christians at Corinth, who were rich, the Macedonians were very poor (2 Cor. 8:2). However, their spirit and practice of giving were exemplary. For this reason, Paul wanted to use this level of generosity to encourage and challenge the Corinthians to give according to their means and blessings as well (2 Cor. 8:11). "For I testify that they gave as much as they were able, and even beyond their ability. Entirely on their own" (2 Cor. 8:3, NIV).

## *Giving to the Needy*

The specific issue that Paul addresses in this Bible passage is the collection of money for the needy believers in Jerusalem. It is important to note that this was a ministry started by the Corinthians, but they had not finished it. "Last year you were the first not only to give but also to have the desire to do so. Now finish the work, so that your eager willingness to do it may be matched by your completion of it, according to your means" (2 Cor. 8:10, 11). In the larger picture of Christian ministry, this is the mission to which God has called His church—to help the poor and to provide for people in need. Jesus underscores this calling with the parable of the sheep and the goats at the end of time (Matt. 25:31-46). The point of the parable is simple: When we do good to others, we are, in fact, doing it to Jesus. What makes the Macedonian Christians stand out in Paul's letter? It was the fact that they wanted to be part of God's mission, despite their extreme poverty.

## *Giving One's Life First to God*

The example of generous giving by the Macedonian churches begs the question: What motivated them to give of their all? The answer, I believe, is wrapped up in their understanding and experience of the grace of God in Christ (2 Cor. 8:1). They had a personal relationship with Jesus; they had tasted the goodness of God; and this grace—flowing freely within them—manifested itself in their willingness and commitment to give of themselves first to the Lord (2 Cor. 8:5). In essence, their acts of generosity were an expression of the grace of God in their lives. The giving of their monetary gifts was an extension of their giving to the Lord. Because they gave themselves first to God, there was no limit to what God could do through them. Stewardship for them had become a way of life—a life of continuous and generous giving to the Lord.

## STEWARDS OF INFLUENCE:
*Agents of Change*

# CHRIST: THE FRAGRANCE OF THE CHRISTIAN LIFE

My son, Jaydon, and I were in the car in COSTCO's parking lot waiting for a vehicle to pull out so we could pull into its space. We assumed that the parked car would be leaving at any moment because the driver had loaded her shopping bags and had returned the trolley. We could see the reverse lights at the rear of the car, which indicated that the driver was ready to drive off. The reality, however, was different. The car was not moving, and I was impatient with the wait. Immediately behind our car were a number of other vehicles waiting for me to move, and, of course, I was waiting for the parked car to pull out. Being aware of other drivers waiting did add to the sense of urgency to do something, even though I knew there was nothing I could do but wait.

The wait felt like an eternity. I started to mumble to myself, expressing my frustration that the parked car was still not moving. Unbeknown to me, Jaydon, who was only 5 and sitting in the back seat, was watching my reaction. He heard the words I was saying. Spontaneously, and unrehearsed, Jaydon calmly said to me, "Daddy, be patient."

Feeling rather disappointed with my reaction to the situation, I responded sheepishly, "I'm sorry, son." At that moment I knew that I had been wrong as a Christian parent. I had behaved in a manner that was contrary to what we have taught our children, and what we expect them to do in similar circumstances. For me, that learning moment was also a reminder of the quiet but powerful impact of the personal influence we all have on others, irrespective of whether our actions and reactions are intentional. Our influence—the way we live and conduct our lives as Christian stewards in the world—can be a positive or negative force that will affect someone's life and choices for now and into the future (2 Cor. 2:15).

## *Personal Influence*

The Bible deals with the issue of personal influence quite extensively. The Christian perspective is highlighted well in 1 Corinthians 10:31-33: "So whether you eat or drink or whatever you do, do it all for the glory of God. Do not cause anyone to stumble, whether Jews, Greeks or the church of God—even as I try to please everyone in every way. For I am not seeking my own good but the good of many so that they may be saved." Paul's counsel to the Christians in Corinth is still valid for us today. We are each part of a community, and it is important that our influence represents Christ. We must keep before us the goal of helping others to experience Jesus and be saved for His eternal kingdom.

## *Parental Influence*

In their sojourn from Egypt to Canaan, Moses continued to remind the Israelites of the importance of loving God fully. Being part of His covenant-keeping people was a total lifetime commitment. It was not limited to only one day of the week—the Sabbath. This emphasis was clearly articulated in these words: "Hear, O Israel: The Lord our God, the Lord is one. Love the Lord your God with all your heart and with all your soul and with all your strength. These commandments that I give you today are to be on your hearts. Impress them on your children. Talk about them when you sit at home and when you walk along the road, when you lie down and when you get up" (Deut. 6:4-7). From the writings of Moses, we see how God desires this message to be communicated and passed on to children, and even to the next generations. In the work of religious education, parents are charged with the spiritual responsibility of leading and influencing their young ones in the way of the Lord. This is Christian stewardship.

## *Influence Does Matter*

The call to accept Jesus as our Savior and Lord is really an invitation to submit every facet of our lives to the rule of His Spirit daily. This is a reminder that as Christians, we do not live our lives in a vacuum or in isolation from other people. What we do, even in private, can influence someone's destiny for eternity. Additionally, we recognize that as stewards and partners with God we are placed here on earth for His purpose, and that purpose is to live out His glory.

# STEWARDS OF COMMUNITY:
## *All My Neighbors*

# ENGAGING STEWARDS

I grew up in a part of the South Pacific region of the world Adventist Church at a time when the church's theological understanding of the "remnant" of Bible prophecy (Rev. 12-14) was often understood to mean separation from all who were not Adventist. Whether this was the correct understanding and application of this biblical concept or not, is not the point. The fact is, at that time Seventh-day Adventists in Samoa often lived out this non-association with the community as a hallmark of their end-time identity. In some extreme cases, this misunderstanding of what Adventism is about led to the church being barred from entering certain villages and districts in Samoa. Many Samoans perceived Seventh-day Adventists as being anti-community and anti-culture. Unfortunately, this perception is not limited to only Samoa and the South Pacific.

## The Mandate to Engage Community

The call and invitation to be God's stewards in the world is quite the opposite of that perception. We are, in fact, mandated by God to be involved and to be engaged with all people—including with those who live "in the world."

"Then God said, 'Let us make mankind in our image, in our likeness, so that they may rule over the fish in the sea and the birds in the sky, over the livestock and all the wild animals, and over all the creatures that move along the ground.' God blessed them and said to them, 'Be fruitful and increase in number; fill the earth and subdue it. Rule over the fish in the sea and the birds in the sky and over every living creature that moves on the ground' " (Gen. 1:28). As members of the human family, and created after the likeness of the Maker Himself, we are to extend His rule—His creativity, His mercy, and His care—to all people with whom we may come in contact. We are called to make a difference within the community and ultimately God's spiritual kingdom, by leading and initiating activities ("be fruitful and increase in number" [vs. 28]) and processes ("fill the earth and subdue it" [vs. 28]). Stewardship is a spiritual responsibility and we have a duty to care for one another. This was God's plan right from the beginning (Gen. 2, 4).

## The Purpose for Community Engagement

When Abraham was called to leave his home and people to go to a foreign place known only to God, it was a call to be involved with other communities. Abraham was to have an outward focus in life, and no longer live for himself. He was to become a steward of God's grace by being a "blessing" to others. "I will make you into a great nation, and I will bless you; I will make your name great, and you will be a blessing. I will bless those who bless you, and whoever curses you I will curse; and all peoples on earth will be blessed through you" (Gen. 12:2, 3).

When God called Jonah to go to Nineveh to proclaim a message of His wrath and ultimate destruction, it was a command to become involved in the lives of people. By God's grace, this engagement would bring about a better outcome. The larger purpose of God for the Ninevites then, and for the people of the world today, was their salvation. "And should I not have concern for the great city of Nineveh, in which there are more than a hundred and twenty thousand people who cannot tell their right hand from their left—and also many animals?" (Jonah 4:11). Jesus expressed this concern for all people of the world in this manner, "In the same way your Father in heaven is not willing that any of these little ones should perish" (Matt. 18:14). Stewardship is about giving people everywhere an opportunity to know about Jesus so that all might be saved. You and I are the links He uses to connect them with Jesus and His kingdom.

## *In the World But Not of This World*

Just prior to His death on the cross, Jesus made it very plain in His prayer what His desire for His disciples was: "I have given them your word and the world has hated them, for they are not of the world any more than I am of the world. My prayer is not that you take them out of the world but that you protect them from the evil one. They are not of the world, even as I am not of it" (John 17:14-16). It is not a decision to lead a life of isolation from people and the world when we make the commitment to accept Jesus as Savior and Lord. Rather, it is a pledge to move forward in faith together with Jesus. This partnership with Him can make a difference in the lives of people wherever we may live as stewards of His kingdom.

## SPECIAL NEEDS STEWARDS:
*Vessels of Honor*

# STEWARDSHIP— MINISTERING TO ALL PEOPLE

My understanding of stewardship was expanded to a large degree because of the influence of two special people in my life. The first was my grandmother, Gagau Uelese, who had not always been blind, but she was the whole time that I knew her. Apart from this physical challenge, Gagau lived a "normal" life. She contributed fully to family and community activities. Growing up, I learned many lessons about life from her. The second person of special influence was my brother Enesi Puni. When he lost his sight it changed not only him but our whole family. These experiences opened a new area of stewardship ministry for me that I had not fully understood nor appreciated before.

## *Gagau Uelese—A Minister of Prayer*

My most memorable time with my grandmother was during the years when my parents were away on their second term as Adventist missionaries. For the next four years I lived with my mother's sister, Fiapai Matau. Often on the weekends my Aunty Fiapai and I would travel by ferry to see my grandmother. I enjoyed these visits a lot, because they provided an opportunity for me to get to know my grandmother better.

What stood out for me during those visits was the fact that my blind grandmother was the first person in her household to wake up early every morning. From inside her mosquito net in her open family "fale" (Samoan word for house), she would start singing a Christian hymn, which was followed by a long prayer. This was her daily routine, and by doing so she was leading out in the family morning devotion. This ritual served as the wake-up call and as an invitation for members of her family to join her in prayer time. She was a devoted Christian with a commitment to prayer. This was her ministry and legacy.

## *Enesi Puni—A Community Leader*

Enesi was a trained pastor and served as an Adventist minister before losing his sight later in life. The ministerial training and his love for Bible study were crucial to Enesi's life after he lost his sight. I remember very well the first time we became aware that Enesi's vision was gone. It was devastating to all of us, but especially to his wife and children. The family's supportive response, however, was very important to Enesi, for it reminded him that he could still be useful despite the blindness, which had brought a major change to his life.

As an extended family, we assisted Enesi and his family to relocate to Auckland, New Zealand, where he was able to receive better support and services from government and nongovernment organizations for his blindness. To ensure that he would continue to have access to study material, we registered Enesi with different entities that provided audiobooks and other resources for the blind. On his own initiative, Enesi enrolled himself in different courses and educational programs offered in Auckland. He received training in Braille and communicated by e-mail with us on a regular basis. In the last few years prior to his death, Enesi was enjoying a good quality of life with his family, and actively participated in the life of his local church and community. He was a certified Samoan translator working on contract with different hospitals in Auckland, and he was a registered marriage celebrant. The way he lived affirmed that special-needs people can minister and are capable of giving back to their communities.

## *Stewardship and Ministry to Special-Needs Groups*

My experience with my grandmother and brother has helped me to think of blind persons as a special people group with particular needs. These are individuals whom Jesus loves and came into this world "to seek and to save" (Luke 19:10). "The Spirit of the Lord is upon Me, because He has anointed Me to preach the gospel to the poor; He has sent Me to heal the brokenhearted, to proclaim liberty to the captives, and recovery of sight to the blind, to set at liberty those who are oppressed; to proclaim the acceptable year of the Lord" (Luke 4:18, 19, NKJV). These personal experiences of living and growing up with family members who were "blind" have created a new awareness in me about my personal responsibility as a steward to these and other special-needs people in the world. Ministering to, and with, special-needs persons must be part of Christian stewardship and the wider mission of the church.

# STEWARDS OF GOD'S TREASURY:
## *Called To Be Accountable*

# BLESSED TO BE A BLESSING

Job's life-experience with God and his response to his personal loss underscore an important reality and truth about wealth and earthly possessions. God owns them all, and they are temporal blessings only. "Naked I came from my mother's womb, and naked I will depart. The Lord gave and the Lord has taken away; may the name of the Lord be praised" (Job 1:21). While this faith-testimony puts the rightful ownership of everything that Job had, including his life, with God, it also highlights the temporal nature of human wealth and the things of this world. They don't last forever and they are not for us to keep. Jesus made this point very clear in the Sermon on the Mount when He said, "Do not store up for yourselves treasures on earth, where moth and rust destroy, and where thieves break in and steal. But store up for yourselves treasures in heaven, where moth and rust do not destroy, and where thieves do not break in and steal" (Matt. 6:19, 20). God's blessings are given to us so we can share them with others; and more important, to invest with Him in His mission on earth—to make disciples of all people groups (Matt. 28:18-20).

## *Tithe and Offerings: Investments With God*

Our tax accountant in Australia is a secular person, and he always questioned the amount of money we give yearly to God through the church. From his perspective, this was a huge cost and unnecessary expense. He saw our "religious donations" in tithe (the Lord's portion in our income) and offerings (our gifts to God) as a liability, and he was concerned that we were not receiving any benefit from such giving. While we respect our accountant's point of view, my wife and I knew why we did what we did and why we continue to return tithe and give freewill offerings even today. Tithe belongs to God. He is the owner of everything by virtue of being the Creator of the world. Tithing is an act of worship. It is a personal expression of our faithfulness to God and the covenant relationship He initiated with us in Jesus Christ. Offerings, on the other hand, are what we choose to give God in gratitude for all that He has done for us and for all of the blessings of life that He showers on us daily. Beyond the "worship" focus of Christian giving, the returning of tithe and the giving of freewill offerings grants us a unique opportunity as Adventists to be part of God's mission. This is a great privilege.

## *Remembering God With our Blessings*

Financial stewardship, as expressed in our giving of offerings and the returning of the Lord's tithe, is one way whereby we remember God as our constant Provider and Sustainer of life. While this reminder and biblical emphasis is not new, it is certainly critical in today's materialistic world where the focus of living is "self," and the accumulation of wealth becomes an obsession and our vocation. Jesus points out the importance of making God the center of life, while exposing the human mistake of trusting only in our wealth when He told the parable of the "rich fool." Earning money through hard work was not the rich farmer's problem; it was his failure to remember God as the giver of all blessings. Jesus concluded by saying, "This is how it will be with anyone who stores up things for himself but is not rich toward God" (Luke 12:21).

## *Sharing God's Blessings With the Poor*

The state of Maryland in the United States, where we live, is supposed to be the "richest" state of this country, with a median household income of US$69,272 according to the US census 2010. Yet, in spite of this wealth, I see very often on the road and at traffic lights individuals who are begging for money. I know that this picture of people asking for help is the reality in countries all over the world. Jesus calls His disciples to respond positively and minister to this need. "The poor you will always have with you" (Matt. 26:11). To the rich young ruler, He said, ". . . go, sell your possessions and give to the poor, and you will have treasure in heaven" (Matt. 19:21). God's purpose for His stewards in the world is not to accumulate wealth and keep it for oneself, but to give as God has given all—in Christ Jesus. Giving our all in response to God's all is the secret of Christian financial stewardship and investment.

# THE STEWARD-LEADER:
*Following God's Lead*

# STEWARD-LEADERS

"As a pastor I cannot lead from a distance. I've got to be present with the people." Pastor Andre Ascalon of the First Seventh-day Adventist Church of Newark, New Jersey (USA), shared this statement with me. It made a real impression. As a pastor he ministers to two congregations, yet he lives two hours away from his churches. Despite the distance, he is always present with his congregations at least twice a week, including prayer meetings. He rarely accepts invitations to preach and teach outside of his churches because he wants to be close and available to his members.

The Newark church has shown impressive growth in both its membership and financial resources. As a result of challenging his members to make their place of worship representative of their God, church facilities have been improved and upgraded. Pastor Ascalon is also committed to helping members extend their ministry to the local community. While there may be many varying factors that contribute to the growth and vibrancy of life in this church, I'm convinced that the steward-leadership of the pastor plays a significant role in the growth experience of this congregation.

## *The Steward-Leader*

The apostle Peter indicated that when Christian leaders administer and exercise their responsibilities, they are doing so on behalf of God Himself, the "Chief Shepherd" (1 Pet. 5:2, 3). The idea of representing God through the gift of leadership is highlighted further in Peter's reference to the biblical concept of "calling" (1 Pet. 5:10). Leaders are in the business of influencing people to live according to God's purpose, which means they are being called to be His agents of positive change in the world. The leader's call to guide God's people is a privilege and an honor but never a right. I saw this demonstrated in the Christian leadership of Pastor Ascalon's ministry.

## *The Shepherd Motif*

In Scripture, steward-leadership finds expression in the imagery of the shepherd and the principles of "shepherding." In fact, Peter seems to understand these two ministry concepts of "stewardship" and "shepherding" as one and the same reality (1 Pet. 5:4). For Peter, Christian leaders (pastors and elders) are shepherds who, on behalf of God, lead "His flock," the church. Shepherds lead from the front. They are "willing" leaders, and they take the initiative to lead and provide direction. They know God has called them to their assigned leadership role. They are assertive, they demonstrate a total commitment to the task, and lead by example (1 Pet. 5:2-4). This is steward-leadership.

## *The Leadership Reality*

Leadership is not without its challenges, and Peter understood this from his own experience. As a result, he reminded elders of the importance of humility in Christian service (1 Pet. 5:5). Humility has to be a "constant" in steward-leadership.

Peter also reminds Christian leaders of Satan's desire to destroy them and those they are leading. But there is good news. In the midst of these tests and sufferings, Peter reminds the steward-leader to "cast all your anxiety on him because he cares for you" (1 Pet. 5:7). Moreover, God's grace is sufficient to restore steward-leaders when they fail. God's grace will make them strong when they are weak, and it will keep them upright and firm when they slide (1 Pet. 5:10).

The beginning and end of steward-leadership is God. Leadership is never a destination but a process where God is continually working out His purposes in our lives. As steward-leaders we are partners with Him. We are not alone. God is with us!